THE TORCHLIGHTERS
ULTIMATE ACTIVITY BOOK

HEROES OF THE FAITH

Presented to:

_____

From:

_____

Executive Editor: Steve Cleary
Managing Editor: Andrea Lyons
Writer: Nancy Persaud
Copy Editor: Traci McConnell
Creative Director: Robert Fernandez
Creative Consultant: Josh Howard

Design and Illustrations by: Herald Entertainment, Inc.

First Printing 2017
Printed in the United States of America

Visit our website at: www.torchlighters.co

ISBN: 978-0-9992893-0-3

Table of Contents

4   Bible Scripture Hebrews 12:1–2

5   Jim Elliot

13   William Tyndale

21   John Bunyan

29   Eric Liddell

37   Gladys Aylward

45   Richard Wurmbrand

53   Perpetua

61   Amy Carmichael

69   William Booth

77   Samuel Morris

85   Augustine

93   Corrie ten Boom

101   John Wesley

109   Robert Thomas

117   Martin Luther

125   Adoniram and Ann Judson

133   Answer & Color Keys

"Therefore, since we are surrounded by so great a cloud of witnesses, let us also lay aside every weight, and sin which clings so closely, and let us run with endurance the race that is set before us, looking to Jesus, the founder and perfecter of our faith, who for the joy that was set before him endured the cross, despising the shame, and is seated at the right hand of the throne of God."

— **Hebrews 12:1–2**

A Man of UNSELFISHNESS

Jim's Story

Jim Elliot and some of his college friends enjoyed working as a team to spread the gospel. One day when they were traveling together, their car stalled on some railroad tracks. Then they saw the train coming! They scrambled out of their vehicle just seconds before the train demolished the car.

After the wreck, Jim told his parents, "It sobered me considerably to think that the Lord kept me from harm in this. Certainly, He has a work that He wants me in somewhere."

Following God's leading, Jim became a missionary after he graduated from college. He traveled to Ecuador to serve God among South American tribal people. After about a year, he married Elisabeth Howard, and their daughter, Valerie, was born while they were serving in Ecuador.

Jim still enjoyed working with a team to spread the gospel. His new teammates and fellow missionaries were Pete Fleming, Nate Saint, Ed McCully, and Roger Youderian.

God gave Jim a strong desire to reach the tribal people. The Waodani, an indigenous people group, had a reputation for violence and suspicion toward outsiders. Together the team prayed and devised a plan to reach out to the Waodani by dropping gifts from their plane. After some initial success in building a relationship with the Waodani, something went terribly wrong. There were those among the Waodani who did not trust the missionaries. They attacked and killed the entire team, after the plane landed on the Waodani beach.

Through the tragedy, God continued moving among the Waodani. After a time, they realized that the missionaries had unselfishly laid down their lives for the tribe. Jim and his team had hoped that they would lead the Waodani to an understanding of Christ's love. In an unexpected way, the missionaries had accomplished that goal. The sacrifice of their lives helped the Waodani understand Jesus' ultimate sacrifice on the cross and led many of the tribe to follow Him.

Key Bible Verse:

"Do nothing from selfish ambition or conceit, but in humility count others more significant than yourselves. Let each of you look not only to his own interests, but also to the interests of others." (Philippians 2:3–4)

Key Word: UNSELFISHNESS

Unselfishness: Generosity, willingness to share, ability to put the needs of others before one's own needs.

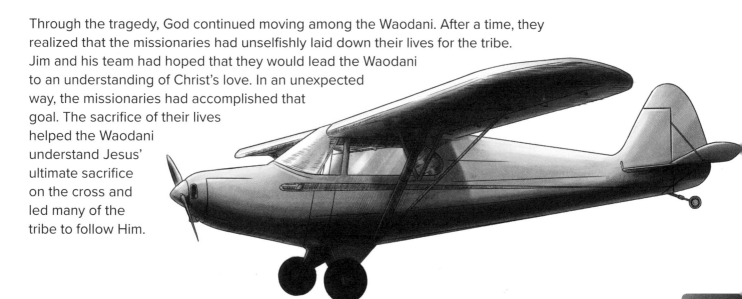

Fascinating Facts!

Close Calls

The train incident wasn't Jim Elliot's first "close call" with danger. Once, while he was hunting, a bullet grazed his hair, barely missing his head.

Encouraging Friends

In college, Jim encouraged his friends to share what they had learned from the Bible each day. He greeted them by saying, "What's your verse for today?" How can you encourage your friends in their walk with God?

The Waodani

The jungle tribe Jim and his friends contacted was known as the Auca tribe. Auca, meaning "savage," was a name used by other tribes as an insult before the tribe was transformed by God's love. Now they are known by the name Waodani, meaning "the people." Their name is also spelled "Waorani" or "Huaorani."

Going Back to the Tribe

Family members, including Jim's wife, Elisabeth, and his daughter, Valerie, returned to the tribe with a message of forgiveness and salvation for the men who had killed their loved ones. Valerie played with the Waodani children, while her mother ministered among the tribe. Many of the Waodani people responded to the sacrificial love of Jesus through these women and gave their lives to Him.

Nate Saint's Son

Nate Saint, a missionary pilot, flew the plane that helped Jim Elliot and the other missionaries reach the Waodani people. After Nate's death, his son, Steve, continued to spend school vacations with his Aunt Rachel, who was a missionary to the Waodani tribe. As a teenager, Steve was baptized by two of the Waodani men who had come to know Christ after killing Steve's father and the other missionaries. Later Steve Saint served as a missionary among the tribe.

A Flying Car

Steve Saint started a company in the United States that invents machines to help people spread the gospel in hard-to-reach areas. One of the machines is a flying car!

Missionary Stamps

The government of Ecuador issued postage stamps honoring Jim and the other missionaries who were martyred for their faith.

Follow the instructions below to find Jim Elliot's motto. What do you think the motto means? In what ways did Jim prove by the way he lived that he believed his motto? The answer is in the Answer Key.

1. Jim Elliot served the Lord in Ecuador, South America. Cross out, in columns B, C, and E, the names of South American countries. (Refer to a map of South America if you need help.)

2. Jim Elliot demonstrated unselfishness. Cross out, in columns A, C, and D, words more than five letters long related to unselfishness.

3. Cross out the two-letter words only in columns B and D.

4. Cross out, in all columns, the first or last names of the five men who were trying to reach the Waodani tribe for Christ.

5. To read Jim Elliot's quote, start at the top of the grid, and going in order from left to right, copy the remaining words onto the dotted lines below the grid.

A	B	C	D	E
HE	FLEMING	BRAZIL	AT	IS
NO	PERU	FOOL	CONSIDERATE	YOUDERIAN
PETE	BY	GENEROUS	OF	CHILE
CARING	WHO	URUGUAY	GIVES	WHAT
HE	WE	CANNOT	IN	ARGENTINA
SAINT	KEEP	MCCULLY	COMPASSIONATE	TO
ED	OF	COLOMBIA	GAIN	JIM
KINDNESS	AT	WHAT	ON	HE
CANNOT	VENEZUELA	SHARING	TO	NATE
ROGER	LOSE	GIVING	THOUGHTFUL	PARAGUAY

"
__ __ __ _____ ___ _____ _____ __ _____

_____ __ _____ _____ __ _____ _____ .
"

The missionaries flew over the jungle to reach the Waodani tribe.

Jim's wife and daughter returned to the Waodani people with a message of
forgiveness and salvation.

Fan Your Gifts into Flame

Jim Elliot's missionary team worked well together to accomplish tasks. Jim was a leader and encourager, and Pete learned building skills. Nate served as a pilot. Ed had studied missionary medicine, and Roger had been a paratrooper and a church pianist.

What kind of missionary could you be?
What gifts has God given you to love and serve Him in missionary work or in other ways? Do you have skills that you can "fan into flame" to prepare you to serve God later?

Put a 1 on the line in front of any statement below that describes you sometimes or a little bit.
Put a 2 if it describes you generally or most of the time.
Put a 3 if it is a very important part of your life.

Leave the line blank if it doesn't describe you at all.

> "For this reason I remind you to fan into flame the gift of God. ..."
>
> — 2 Timothy 1:6

To fan something into flame means to make it more intense, or stronger.

___ I like to organize groups for games or tasks. **A**
___ I like to invite people to church or Bible study. **E**
___ I am willing to try different kinds of food. **P**
___ I like to care for animals, or for younger children, or others who need help. **K**
___ I like to learn new things from the Bible and other sources to share with others. **T**
___ I plan ahead or make lists to help me manage my time. **A**
___ I am comfortable talking to people about my faith. **E**
___ I am concerned about people who don't know Jesus. **E**
___ Others look to me for help when they don't understand something. **T**
___ I am concerned about the poor and the unreached people. **K**
___ I pray for the needs of others. **K**
___ I like to go to places I have never been before. **P**
___ I can motivate others to greater service for the Lord. **A**
___ I like to meet new people and learn about different cultures. **P**
___ I can patiently explain new skills and ideas to others. **T**

Missionary Gifts and Ministry
Add up the total numbers for each letter above (A, E, T, P and K) and enter the numbers below to see how your gifts might be used for the mission field. The higher the number the stronger your gifting!

____ **A = Administrator: Able to organize and handle detailed plans**

____ **E = Evangelist: A messenger of the Good News of the gospel**

____ **T = Teacher: Teaches and disciples others**

____ **P = Pioneer: Willing to go to new places and start new things**

____ **K = Kindness (Compassion): Able to assist those in need**

Which section has the highest total? For example, if the "Teacher" section best describes you, you could offer to teach a class of younger children at your church. What else could you do to fan your gifts into flame?

What Do You Think?

Read the facts about Jim Elliot's life below, and write your thoughts about the questions on the lines provided. Include any thoughts on selfishness or unselfishness that come to mind.

1. Jim was on the school wrestling team. Like Eric Liddell, he was a strong competitor. Should Christians ever let others win at games and sports, or should they always try their hardest? Is it possible to do your best and still be unselfish?

   _____

   _____

2. When Jim received poor grades at school one semester, he told his parents that he thought studying God's Word was more important than his school subjects. What do you think of his reason for getting poor grades? What do you think his parents' response to him might have been?

   _____

   _____

3. After his death, Jim's wife, Elisabeth, and his daughter, Valerie, returned to share a message of God's forgiveness with the Waodani tribe. Do you think Jim would have wanted them to do so? Can you think of a verse from God's Word to support what you think?

   _____

   _____

4. Jim and his friends worked in a place they knew was extremely dangerous. Should missionaries work in dangerous places? Why or why not?

   _____

   _____

5. Although Jim and the other missionaries had guns which they fired in the air as a warning, they did not use them to defend themselves against the spear-wielding Waodani attackers. Do you think the missionaries should have defended themselves? What was the missionaries' eternal destiny? What was the attackers' eternal destiny at that time?

   _____

   _____

Losing and Gaining

"He is no fool who gives what he cannot keep to gain what he cannot lose," Jim Elliot wrote in his journal the year he graduated from college. (A fool is someone who acts in a way that is not wise.) How would you share this quote with someone else in your own words?

_____

_____

Cross out anything on the list below that Jim gave up to follow God's call to Ecuador. Circle anything that he would never have to give up.

1. A comfortable house in America
2. Joy in the knowledge that he helped people come to know Christ
3. Frequent visits with friends and relatives at home
4. Safety
5. His life on earth
6. God's love
7. The example he left for others in living a life of obedience to God
8. Opportunities for higher paying jobs in America
9. Freedom from guilt for his sins
10. Hope for eternity

Are there things that Jim gave up that would have lasted forever if he had kept them? Would he have been able to keep them in eternity? Jim gave up what he would not be able to keep and gained what he could never lose.

The Bible says, "Set your minds on things that are above, not on things on earth." (Colossians 3:2)

Does Jim's quote agree with this verse?

John 12:24 (NIV) says, "Very truly I tell you, unless a kernel of wheat falls to the ground and dies, it remains only a single seed. But if it dies, it produces many seeds."

How was that verse true in the life of Jim Elliot?

Trusting Jesus as our Lord and Savior means giving up our right to have control of our lives and turning our rights and all control over to Him. Like Jim Elliot, when we trust the Lord, we pay less attention to things that we can't keep and more attention to things that we can't lose.

Matthew 6:19–21

"Do not lay up for yourselves treasures on earth, where moth and rust destroy and where thieves break in and steal, but lay up for yourselves treasures in heaven, where neither moth nor rust destroys and where thieves do not break in and steal. For where your treasure is, there your heart will be also."

A Man of PERSEVERANCE

William's Story

In England in the 1500s, most parents could not read the Christmas story from the Bible to their children. Parents were not allowed to teach their children the Lord's Prayer or the Ten Commandments in English, because it was against the law. Children did not learn the 23rd Psalm or any other Bible verses in English.

At the time, only a few people in England could read the Bible, at all. It was available to them only in Latin, and most of the people could speak and read only English.

Church leaders did not want the Bible to be translated into English. They thought less educated people would not understand the Scriptures and that their misunderstanding would lead them to follow false teachings.

But translator William Tyndale loved God's Word and yearned to make it available to everyone. He persevered in his plan to translate the Bible from the original Hebrew and Greek into English, even when the plan angered important people.

He once told a church official, "If God spare my life ... I will cause a boy that driveth the plough shall know more of the Scripture than thou dost."

That kind of talk got William into trouble with the government and the church. As he secretly worked on his translation, he avoided capture by moving from one location to another. He persevered in his work. Finally, in 1526, his English New Testament was printed in Germany. William smuggled copies into England by ship, in bales of cotton.

The King of England opposed his work, and the church responded by ordering the New Testament to be burned. In addition, William lost the translation of several books in a shipwreck and had to rewrite them.

William was betrayed by a "friend," arrested and sentenced to death. His final words were, "Lord, open the King of England's eyes." His prayer was answered a year after his death, when King Henry VIII authorized the Scriptures to be translated and printed in English.

Key Bible Verses:

"Therefore, since we are surrounded by such a great cloud of witnesses, let us throw off everything that hinders and the sin that so easily entangles. And let us run with perseverance the race marked out for us." (Hebrews 12:1, NIV)

Key Word: PERSEVERANCE

Perseverance: Diligence and determination in completing something despite difficulties or delays

John 1:1 in the original Greek

Ἐν ἀρχῇ ἦν ὁ λόγος, καὶ ὁ λόγος ἦν πρὸς τὸν θεόν, καὶ θεὸς ἦν ὁ λόγος.

John 1:1 in Latin

in principio erat Verbum et Verbum erat apud Deum et Deus erat Verbum

William Tyndale's translation

In the beginnynge was the worde and the worde was with God: and the worde was God.
– Tyndale Bible

✓ **Henry Phillips**

Henry Phillips pretended he was William's friend so he could betray William to the authorities. His betrayal led to William's capture. (Who betrayed Jesus in a way that led to His capture?)

✓ **Danger**

Parents in England had been arrested for teaching their children the Lord's Prayer and the Ten Commandments in English. William knew the danger of making the Bible available in English. It was against the law to write or even own any portion of a Bible in English. Today, though, we have the freedom to learn the Ten Commandments in English. How many can you name?

✓ **Extreme Handwriting**

William had finished translating the New Testament and part of the Old Testament when Genesis, Exodus, Leviticus, Numbers, and Deuteronomy (the Pentateuch) were destroyed in a shipwreck. He had to rewrite them by hand — more than 150,000 words!

✓ **Answered Prayer**

William's final prayer before he entered eternity was for the king. One year later, in 1537, King Henry VIII approved the printing of the Bible in English.

✓ **Not Many Left**

Thousands of copies of William's New Testament were distributed in England. Fewer than five first editions exist today.

✓ **Image to Color**

A monogram is a design using a person's initials. William Tyndale's monogram appeared in the Matthew's Bible, published in the year after William's death. The monogram recognized William's contribution to the making of the English Bible.

After William smuggled his New Testament into England, furious authorities devised a plan to keep people from reading it. They bought many of the books to prevent others from having them. Then, they burned them! However, copies still made it into the hands of eager seekers. The money from the authorities' purchases helped support William while he continued doing the difficult translation work they opposed.

Solve the cryptogram to read one of the verses from the New Testament that William translated. *Here are two big hints:* **The letter "T" below stands for "E" and the word "PERSEVERANCE" appears twice. The answer is in the Answer Key and is found in Romans 5:3–4 (NIV).**

‾‾ ‾‾‾‾ ‾‾‾‾ ‾‾ ‾‾‾ ‾‾‾‾‾‾‾‾‾
VT ZXMG IXGNS KU GYN MYHHTNKUIM

‾‾‾‾‾‾ ‾‾ ‾‾‾‾ ‾‾‾‾ ‾‾‾‾‾‾‾‾
CTWZYMT VT AUGV PJZP MYHHTNKUI

‾‾‾‾‾‾‾ ‾‾‾‾‾‾‾‾‾‾‾
RNGEYWTM RTNMTBTNZUWT;

‾‾‾‾‾‾‾‾‾‾‾ ‾‾‾‾‾‾‾‾‾
RTNMTBTNZUWT, WJZNZWPTN;

‾‾‾ ‾‾‾‾‾‾‾‾‾ ‾‾‾‾
ZUE WJZNZWPTN, JGRT.

William avoided capture by moving from place to place.

Make a Feather Quill Pen

In William Tyndale's time, people wrote with quill pens made from feathers. Use the instructions below to make your own feather quill pen.

Needed: Turkey feathers (available at craft stores); a craft knife or other sharp cutting tool; an adult experienced in using cutting tools safely; a toothpick; and calligraphy ink.

1. Starting about an inch from the tip of the feather, slice off the tip of the feather at a 45-degree angle. (Note: You may want to use plastic drinking straws or additional turkey feathers to practice cutting the tip into the proper shape.) Using a toothpick, clean the feather membranes out a few inches from the inside of the feather's shaft.
2. Make a slit about 1/8 inch long in the center of the longer end of the tip. The slit will help the pen hold ink.
3. Whittle the tip with the cutting tool to form a shape that resembles the tip of a fountain pen.
4. On a cutting board or other hard surface, trim off the pointed end of the tip.

1/8 inch

5. Remove about 4 to 5 inches of the feather barbs to make a comfortable quill for your hand.

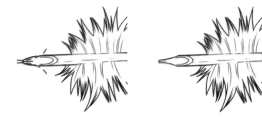 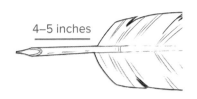

4–5 inches

6. Dip the quill in ink. Gently brush off the end of the quill on the top rim of the bottle to remove excess ink.
7. Holding it at a 45- to 90-degree angle, write with the pen, dipping it in ink again after every four or five letters. Your quill pen writing will improve with practice.

Suggested verses to write:

Romans 10:17, Psalm 119:105, John 5:39, 1 John 5:11, 2 Timothy 3:16, Isaiah 40:8, Matthew 24:35, Jeremiah 23:29, Luke 24:25

Hiding Scripture
William Tyndale and the readers of his English Bible had to hide their copies of Scripture. Using your quill pen, write Bible verses on index cards or pieces of paper. Where would you hide the verses if you didn't want anyone to find them? Hide the verses in different places in your room or classroom.

What Do You Think?

William Tyndale was a Bible smuggler, hiding English Bibles in bales of cotton and other goods. William was breaking the laws of England by providing people with Bibles.

Should Christians ever break the law?

Read each pair of ideas below, and decide which one in each pair is the most important consideration in deciding whether Christians should smuggle Bibles into countries where the Bible is illegal. Write your thoughts on the line below each pair.

1. • The Bible says, "Let every person be subject to the governing authorities" (Romans 13:1). This verse means that Christians must not take Bibles into countries where government leaders do not want Bibles.

   • Christ commanded His followers, "Go into all the world and proclaim the gospel to the whole creation" (Mark 16:15). "All the world" includes countries where it is illegal to preach the gospel. In that case, "We must obey God rather than men" (Acts 5:29).

   _____

2. • Christians must obey all the laws and commands of rulers, even if those laws cause them to disobey God's Word.

   • The following people in the Bible disobeyed government rulers in order to obey God: Moses' mother, Rahab, Daniel, the apostles, and others.

   _____

3. • Christians should show respect and tolerance for the beliefs of those who don't follow Christ. Giving them Bibles does not show respect for their beliefs.

   • When we tell others the Good News of the way to eternal life, we are demonstrating our extreme love for them. Jesus said, "I am the way, and the truth, and the life. No one comes to the Father except through me" (John 14:6).

   _____

Research
Find out the names of five countries where owning or sharing Bibles is still illegal today.

Learning to Persevere

"You won't believe what my dad said!" Seth reported to his friends at school one day. "He said I can't play soccer if I get any grades below a C!"

"It must be dumb parent week," Nicole joined in from the other end of the lunch table. "My mom wants me to learn to mow the lawn starting this Saturday!"

Everyone looked at Hannah. She always had something disrespectful to say about her parents or teachers that made her classmates laugh. She prayed silently for strength. "I just don't have anything interesting to say today," she said. A few of her classmates groaned, but they moved onto another topic. "Thank you, God," she prayed.

The leader at Hannah's Bible study group had challenged the group to make a commitment for the next week on following Philippians 2:14, "Do all things without grumbling or disputing." It seemed like an impossible task for Hannah. She was always grumbling and complaining.

But she decided to ask God to forgive her and help her change.

That night, God did something that put Hannah's commitment to the test. Hannah's parents told her to give them her phone every night after supper until her homework and chores were completed. Hannah normally would have grumbled and complained, even though she knew she wasted too much time on her phone.

She asked God for strength, then handed over her phone, smiled, and walked quietly to her room.

Her mom and dad were amazed. She heard them talking to each other, and her mom even called a friend and talked to her about Hannah's new attitude. She would tell her classmates at school about depending on God to change her heart and help her persevere in overcoming "grumbling and complaining," but not yet. She needed more experience depending on God for strength to obey and persevere no matter what.

To think about:

Why did Hannah want to wait before telling her classmates about what she was doing? How might they react when she tells them she no longer wants to complain about her parents?

Should Hannah have told her parents about her plan?

What obstacles did William Tyndale face? How do you think he was able to persevere?

A Man of TRUST

John's Story

At the age of 9, John Bunyan had already earned a bad reputation in Elstow, England, where he lived. John's parents could not control him, and he couldn't control himself!

Secretly, John knew that he was not pleasing God. Finally, he left home at about age 16 and joined the army. One day, he switched duties with another soldier, and an enemy's bullet struck the other soldier. God had spared him from danger, and he began to believe God wanted him alive for a reason.

John left the army and got married when he was 19. He and his wife were very poor. They didn't have "so much as a dish or a spoon betwixt us both," John wrote. But his wife served as a godly influence in his life.

Then, when John was about 21, he met three ladies who were full of joy and peace because of putting their trust in Jesus. The women and their pastor encouraged John to trust the One who saves those who cannot save themselves. "Your own works can't save you," the pastor explained. John listened to him and trusted completely in the Lord.

Full of joy, John began to share his faith with others. Preaching outside an official government church was against the law; consequently, John went to jail. While in jail, he began to write a story about a Christian pilgrim who struggles, but because of God's great grace remains on the narrow path to heaven.

In 1678, a few years after John's release from jail, he took *The Pilgrim's Progress* to a printer and said, "I have a book of little worth." That book became one of the best-selling books of all time. Since the first printing of *The Pilgrim's Progress*, it has been translated into over 200 languages and distributed around the world.

Key Bible Verse:

"Trust in the LORD with all your heart, and do not lean on your own understanding. In all your ways acknowledge him, and he will make straight your paths."
(Proverbs 3:5–6)

Key Word: TRUST

Trust: A firm belief in the truth, dependability, power, or strength of someone or something

Fascinating Facts!

The Plague and Trust

The Great Plague was an epidemic of the bubonic plague that occurred in England in 1665 and 1666. Thousands died from the disease. The jailer released John temporarily during the plague, but told him to return. At other times, the jailer let John out of "gaol" (the archaic British spelling for "jail") for brief periods, knowing that he was trustworthy and would return.

Tinker by Trade

During the 17th century, two centuries before goods were manufactured, if anything broke it would be mended if at all possible. The tinker was a well respected trade, and a tinker's skills were much in demand. The tinker's ability to work with all kinds of metal meant that most metal objects, such as pots, pans, cooking utensils, or metal parts could be repaired on site.

John Bunyan is likely the most famous tinker of the 17th century. John served in the Parliament Army during the English Civil War and his skills would undoubtedly have been used in maintaining the garrison equipment.

John's Family

John's first wife died before he went to jail. She and John had four children. The oldest, Mary, was born blind. John and his second wife, Elizabeth, had two children that lived. Elizabeth worked hard to help John and win his release from jail. Mary often brought soup to John's jail cell to encourage him. John was deeply grieved when Mary died at the age of 13 while he was in jail. His grief led him to begin work on a book titled *The Resurrection of the Dead*.

Shoelaces

To help support his family, John made shoelaces in his jail cell and sold them from his cell window to people passing by the jail. He said he sold "many hundred gross." (A gross is 12 dozen.)

Bunyan's Burial

John Bunyan is buried in a graveyard near London, England, called Bunhill Fields. Others buried there include Susanna Wesley, mother of John Wesley; Daniel Defoe, author of *Robinson Crusoe*; and Isaac Watts, the beloved hymn writer.

Bedford jail where John Bunyan was imprisoned

The Full Armor of God
Ephesians 6:10–20

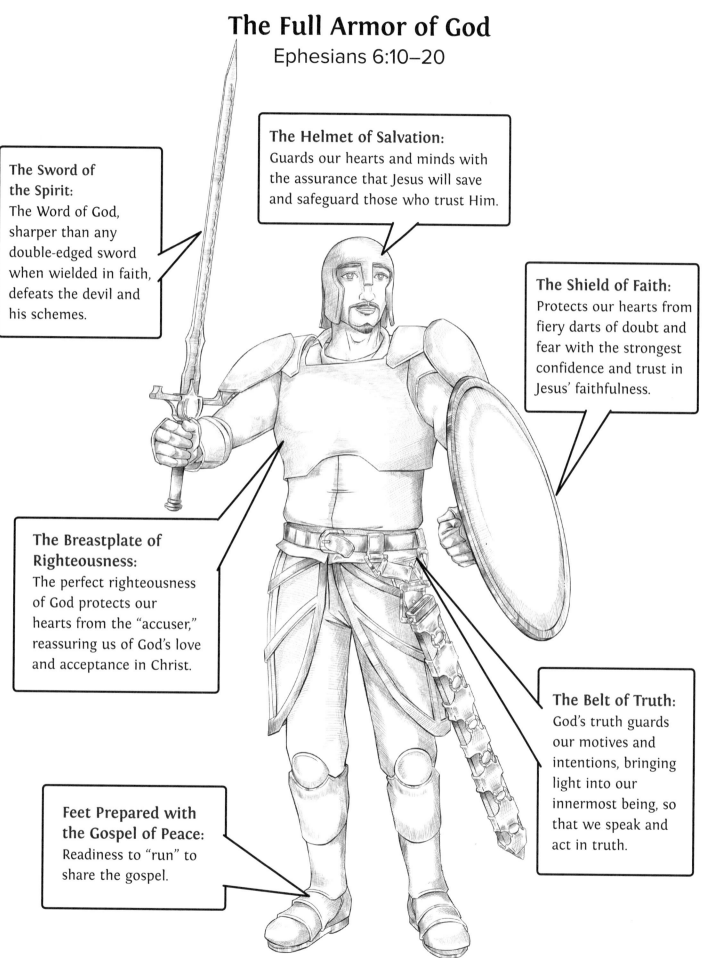

The Sword of the Spirit:
The Word of God, sharper than any double-edged sword when wielded in faith, defeats the devil and his schemes.

The Helmet of Salvation:
Guards our hearts and minds with the assurance that Jesus will save and safeguard those who trust Him.

The Shield of Faith:
Protects our hearts from fiery darts of doubt and fear with the strongest confidence and trust in Jesus' faithfulness.

The Breastplate of Righteousness:
The perfect righteousness of God protects our hearts from the "accuser," reassuring us of God's love and acceptance in Christ.

The Belt of Truth:
God's truth guards our motives and intentions, bringing light into our innermost being, so that we speak and act in truth.

Feet Prepared with the Gospel of Peace:
Readiness to "run" to share the gospel.

Color the image of Christian, from *The Pilgrim's Progress*.

THE INTERPRETER'S HOUSE

SALVATION HILL

THE GATE

LEGALITY HILL

THE SWAMP OF DESPONDENCY

APOLLYON'S LAIR

THE CITY OF DESTRUCTION

THE HOUSE BEAUTIFUL

THE CELESTIAL CITY

THE VALLEY OF HUMILIATION

THE PLEASANT HILLS

VANITY FAIR

CASTLE DESPAIR

Christian's journey

Pilgrim's Armor

Christian, the main character in John Bunyan's, *The Pilgrim's Progress*, faced daunting obstacles on his perilous journey toward the Celestial City. The Lord provided Christian and other pilgrims with armor made up of a sword, shield, helmet, breastplate, "all-prayer," and shoes that would not wear out.

Read Ephesians 6:13–18.

What parts of the armor of God mentioned in those verses are similar to Christian's armor in *The Pilgrim's Progress*?

Make a Helmet

Needed: At least 2 pieces of craft foam, poster board, or construction paper measuring approximately 17 x 12 inches; pen, pencil, or marker; scissors; glue; one or two long-pronged brads.

- Overlap the short ends of two pieces of the craft foam or other material about 1 inch and staple them together. Wrap it around a "pilgrim's" head to size it. Leave 1 to 2 more inches than needed to fit snugly, and cut off the rest. (Don't staple the other end yet.)
- Cut off a strip of the helmet on one of the long ends to leave the helmet about 9 inches tall. Measure off and draw a line across the bottom of the helmet about 1 ½ inches from the bottom edge all the way around.
- Measure and mark off 1 ½ inch strips from the top to the bottom of the helmet all the way around above the line you drew. (It doesn't matter if you end up with one narrower strip.)
- Cut the strips from the top of the helmet, stopping at the line. Leave every other strip 7 ½ inches tall, and trim every other strip to make it 6 inches tall.
- Overlap the open ends of the helmet 1 or 2 inches, and staple it shut.
- First fold all the 6 inch strips slightly toward the inner center of the helmet. Then fold all the 7 ½ inch strips down on top of the 6 inch strips and secure only the 7 ½ inch strips with one or two long-pronged brads.
- Cut a nose guard and glue it to the front of the helmet. (See the drawing.)

We know that when John Bunyan was a young man, he enjoyed playing a game called "tipcat" and engaging in other pastimes, but sometime he felt guilty for doing so. Is it okay for Christians to play games? What do you think?

_____

Most Christians today believe they can play games that encourage good behavior and build character. Some Christians use sports and games as an opportunity to witness about their faith to non-Christian players. What do you think?

_____

How Much Is Too Much?

When is watching or playing games a distraction from more important activities? An American pastor said, "Anyone who spends more time playing video games than seeking God in prayer has no right to call Jesus, Lord." What do you think of the pastor's statement? (Read some Bible verses about prayer in 1 Thessalonians 5:17, Matthew 6:7, and Matthew 6:9–13.)

_____

In the 1500s, King Henry VIII of England banned a number of games because he believed they would distract his soldiers from their duties. Do you think it would be wise for government leaders to tell people how much time they could spend on sports and games? Is it effective for parents and teachers to make rules about playing games at home or in class? What do you think?

_____

What games do you like to play or watch others play?

_____

Do any of those games ever take time away from your Bible reading, prayer, homework, household chores, commitments, or opportunities to serve others?

_____

Make a Rule

What do you think would be a good rule for time allowed to spend on games? (For example, "I can play games for 30 minutes after my homework is done, if it's not time for bed yet.")

_____

_____

Proverbs 3:5–6

"Trust in the LORD with all your heart, and do not lean on your own understanding. In all your ways acknowledge him, and he will make straight your paths."

As a boy, John Bunyan often did whatever he pleased. He broke rules and laws, and he led other boys to do the same. He thought if he could do anything he wanted, he would have fun, enjoy himself, and feel good. But it didn't work. He was mostly miserable, and he had no peace.

After John trusted in Christ to rule his life and went to prison, he was in a dismal situation. The jail was gloomy, and it smelled bad. Rats shared his cell with him, and he did not have decent food. He missed his family and worried about their well-being. But John continued to trust God, Who had saved him, and the Lord brought him peace and joy. He prayed, read the Bible, talked with other prisoners about God, and wrote books to help others come to know and love God more.

Romans 8:28 tells us, "And we know that for those who love God all things work together for good, for those who are called according to his purpose." John's book *The Pilgrim's Progress* illustrated that both followers of Jesus and those who don't follow Him have struggles. But only Christians can trust that all things, even their struggles, will work for good.

We don't always get to see the results of trusting God during our lifetime. Hebrews 11 lists faithful servants of God through the ages. Then Hebrews 11:39–40 tells us, "All of them pleased God because of their faith! But still they died without seeing what had been promised, since God provided something better for us, so that only together with us would they be made perfect."

Do you think the women who told John Bunyan, a humble tinker, about rest in Jesus knew that he would become the author of one of the best-selling Christian books ever written? God used their trust and obedience, as he uses our faith in Him to bring about His will for the increase of His kingdom.

Christians do not need to seek out difficult experiences. But when painful things come into our lives, we can trust the God who promises to "make all things work together for good, for those who are called according to his purpose."

Trust and obey, for there's no other way, To be happy in Jesus, but to trust and obey.

— Lyrics of a Christian hymn

Do you trust Him?

Eric Liddell
(1902 – 1945)

A Man of SACRIFICE

Eric's Story

Eric Liddell didn't look much like a champion when he ran, and people mocked his strange running style. But he was the fastest runner in all of Scotland. He had become a national hero, and his countrymen waited with eager anticipation to see him compete at the 1924 Olympics in Paris, where Eric was expected to win the gold medal.

Eric did his best to win races, but he had a greater goal. Following his parents' example and God's call, he planned to be a missionary to China. Jesus was far more important to him than the Olympics.

As the time for the Olympics approached, Eric announced that he would not run the 100-meter sprint — his best event! The trials for the race were scheduled on Sunday. Eric had always set aside the Lord's Day for rest and worship. He felt it would dishonor the Lord to run on the Lord's Day, so he faced the monarch of Great Britain with his decision.

The people of Scotland were furious! Eric had crushed their hopes for a win for their country. It seemed to Scotland that Eric was disgracing his country and refusing victory, fame, and glory.

Eric competed in the 200-meter and 400-meter races, instead of in his usual race. Though these had never been his best events, Eric surprised the world by winning the gold medal and setting a new world record in the 400-meter event. He also won a bronze medal in the 200-meter.

Because he was a hero, people listened to Eric, and he used every opportunity to witness about his faith in Christ. He sacrificed his comfortable life in Scotland to serve, with his wife, as a missionary in China for 20 years. Then, as World War II reached them, Eric sacrificed the opportunity to leave China, staying instead to help the wounded and to share his faith. Eric died in China in 1945.

Key Bible Verse:

"Therefore, I urge you, brothers and sisters, in view of God's mercy, to offer your bodies as a living sacrifice, holy and pleasing to God—this is your true and proper worship."
(Romans 12:1, NIV)

Key Word: SACRIFICE

Sacrifice: Giving up something that is prized for the sake of something else considered to be of higher importance.

Great Britain is made up of England, Scotland, and Wales.

How do you think American football fans would react if one of the teams in the Super Bowl refused to play because the game takes place on Sunday?

A Missionary Family

✓ Eric was born in 1902. Many people in America, Scotland, and other Western countries believed that the 1900s would see no more wars, sickness, and poverty. They thought education and technology would conquer serious problems. Even Christians were optimistic, but they understood that people have a problem with sin from which only Jesus can save us. They continued their missionary work around the world. Eric's parents were among the missionaries.

✓ Eric had two brothers, Robert and Ernest, and a sister, Jenny. At age 5, Eric began attending a boarding school in England for children of missionaries. Eric was an excellent athlete during his school days.

> **Internment Camp**
>
> A prison camp, often used during wartime, where the government imprisons people from enemy nations or who could be a threat to them.

✓ A classmate described Eric as "lion-hearted but always modest." What do you think he meant?

✓ Eric never prayed to win a race; he prayed that God would be glorified by the event.

✓ Eric's nickname was "the flying Scotsman" because he ran so fast.

✓ On the day of the 400-meter race that hardly anyone expected Eric to win, someone handed him a note that said, "Them that honor Me, I will honor" (from 1 Samuel 2:30, KJV). How did Eric honor God? How was Eric honored? (See "Eric's Story" on the previous page.)

✓ Eric served as a missionary teacher in China, teaching Chinese students and leading students in athletic activities. He and his wife had three daughters, Patricia, Heather, and Maureen. But he never saw Maureen, because she was born after he died.

✓ During World War II, Japanese soldiers took over the area where Eric worked. By that time, he had sent his wife and two daughters to Canada for safety. Foreigners, including Eric, were sent to internment camps. Eric was friendly and encouraging to others in the camp, but gradually became weaker under the poor conditions. His family received a telegram about his death several weeks after he died. The war ended six months later.

✓ Eric's story was featured in a popular 1981 movie, *Chariots of Fire*.

The ancient Olympians used a flame to remember acts of their mythical gods. The torch remains a part of modern Olympic ceremonies. In some instances, in the Bible, God is revealed through fire, as to Moses in the burning bush and to Israelites in a pillar of fire.

Start at the bottom and find your way through the maze in the burning torch!

In the dust of defeat as well as the laurels of Victory THERE IS A GLORY to be found if one has done HIS BEST.

Eric's quote

Eric unexpectedly won a gold medal in the 400-meter race.

Missionaries sometimes have to learn games and customs that are new to them. Try the variations of the following games from Asia.

Sepak Takraw

Sepak takraw is like volleyball, except the players cannot use their hands to hit the ball. Championship players are very good at striking the ball with their feet. The game goes by different names and has different rules depending on the location in Asia where it is played.

Variation 1

With another player, or with two teams, try hitting a balloon back and forth across a rope or string to each other without using your hands or arms.

Variation 2

Tap a ball, balloon, hacky sack, or bean bag into the air lightly with your foot. See how many times you can bounce it off your foot before it hits the ground.

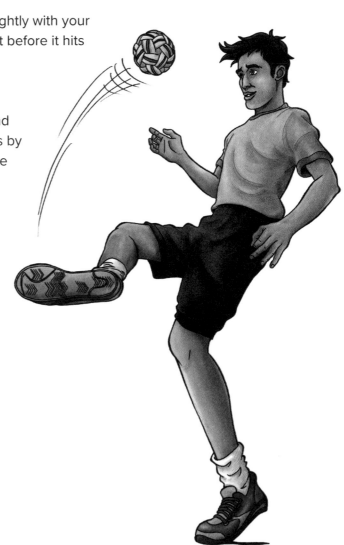

Challenging Variation

Divide into two teams. Each team forms its own circle, and each team has a balloon. One player on each team starts by tapping the balloon into the air with their feet two or more times. The player then gently passes the balloon to another player on the same team with their foot. The second player taps the balloon in the air with their foot two times and passes it also.

Each time the balloon is hit and passed successfully without the balloon hitting the ground, the team gets 5 points. If the balloon is dropped or caught with the hands, the game starts over with the next player in the circle, but the team continues adding to their previous score. The team with the highest score at the end of 10 minutes wins.

What Do You Think?

Eric Liddell made three important decisions that changed his life.

- He decided not to run a race in his best Olympic event because it was on a Sunday. His decision angered and disappointed many in his country, including the monarch of Great Britain.

- Eric decided to stop competing in big races and sacrificed a life of fame to be a missionary in China.

- Eric decided to stay in China during the war, sacrificing his health and life to help the people there.

Do you think he made the right decisions? Why or why not? *(Write your thoughts on the lines below.)*

_____

_____

Do you ever have difficult decisions to make?

What would you do in the following situations — or what would you tell a friend in that situation if they asked for your advice?

Two of your friends are planning to play a mean trick on a classmate. The classmate seems to have no friends in the class. You want to be loyal to your friends, but you feel sorry for the friendless classmate. What would you do?

_____

Your parents don't allow you to go to the park on your own, even though it's right on your block. One day you hear a scream and see an 11-year-old girl fall off the top of the slide. You don't see anyone else in the park. What would you do?

_____

After months of saving, you finally have enough money to get the skateboard you've been wanting to buy. Then a missionary visits your church and talks about kids in another country who have no Bibles and have never heard of Jesus. The price of your skateboard could buy dozens of Bibles. What would you do?

_____

Your decisions today may not have the same kinds of consequences as Eric's decisions. But learning to make hard decisions today, based on your faith in Jesus, will increase your faith for the decisions you will make in the future.

A Living Sacrifice

Have you ever heard the saying, "Be true to yourself"?

What do you think of the saying? Is it biblical advice? What does it mean to be "true to yourself"?

Jesus said, "If anyone would come after me, let him deny himself and take up his cross daily and follow me" (Luke 9:23). Another way of saying this is, "If people want to follow me, they must give up the things they want. They must be willing to give up their lives daily to follow me" (Luke 9:23, NCV).

Romans 12:1 (NIV) says, "Therefore, I urge you, brothers and sisters, in view of God's mercy, to offer your bodies as a living sacrifice, holy and pleasing to God—this is your true and proper worship."

Do those verses encourage us to be true to ourselves?

People "sacrifice" when they give up something that they want for the sake of something else they believe is more important. Eric Liddell sent his family to a safer place, but he stayed in China regardless of the danger. His health, life, and family were valuable to him, but they were not as important to him as God's call to serve and witness to the people of China. Do you think he was true to himself, or did he deny himself?

Keep a log of what you do for a day. Did you get out of bed when you wanted to sleep longer? Did you complete tasks without complaining or arguing? Did you stay with your chores until they were done, instead of getting distracted by entertainment or something else? Did you sacrifice anything you wanted?

To Think About

- If you ever do things you should do instead of what you feel like doing, are you being "true to yourself"?

- Do you agree with the quote, "Most of the world's work is done by people who don't feel like doing it"?

- Can you ever deny yourself and be true to yourself at the same time?

If you think about Christians enjoying unbroken fellowship with God in heaven for eternity, are Christians actually being true to themselves when they sacrifice earthly desires to obey God's call?

A Woman of HUMILITY

Gladys' Story

Gladys Aylward didn't think much about what God wanted her to do with her life. When she was a teenager in England, she liked to smoke, gamble, and go to wild parties. Her goal in life was to become an actress.

Then Gladys attended a revival where she heard the preacher talk about God's love for her and how Jesus came to save the world from sin. She humbly repented of her selfish ways and trusted in Jesus as her Lord and Savior. Her plans and habits changed dramatically.

As Gladys grew to love and trust God more and more, she was saddened by the fact that millions of people in the world had never heard of Jesus. She believed that God was calling her to share the Good News of the gospel with people in China.

But mission agencies would not help her raise the money she needed to go. So Gladys humbly worked as a housemaid until she had the funds to go on her own.

Gladys traveled to China by train and boat.

In China, Gladys helped an older missionary operate an inn where they shared Bible stories with merchants and drivers who passed through the area.

Then, a local leader appointed Gladys as a foot inspector, to help end the torturous custom of foot binding. As a foot inspector, Gladys unbound the girls' feet and shared the story of Jesus' love with many Chinese people.

After eight years of serving in China, Gladys' village came under attack by Japanese soldiers. Villagers had left their children in her care. Though Gladys was wounded in an attack, more than 100 children were depending on her to lead them out of danger. In the middle of the night, the ragged group began a three-week, 100-mile trek across the mountains.

Gladys led the children to safety, encouraging them to persevere in the face of danger, hunger, and exhaustion by singing songs and telling stories of God's faithfulness to His children.

Key Bible Verse:

"Do nothing from selfish ambition or conceit, but in humility count others more significant than yourselves."
(Philippians 2:3)

Key Word: HUMILITY

Humility: The quality of being meek and modest. Humbleness.
Not prideful or showing off. Humble people do not believe that they are better than others or too important to serve others.

Chinese Words

Gladys had to learn Chinese to work in China.
Here is how to say some words in Chinese:

English	How to Say it in Chinese*
Hello	Nee-how
I love Jesus	Woh ai yeh-soo ("Ai" is like the English word "eye")
Jesus loves me	Yeh-soo ai woh
Thank you	Shee shee

pronunciations are approximate

Hudson Taylor's Gospel Lesson

Hudson Taylor served as a missionary to China before Gladys Aylward. Many of his listeners had never heard the gospel, so Taylor used the characters in Chinese writing to teach Bible stories.

Taylor illustrated the story of Christ's death on the cross with the Chinese character for the word "come." The character has a cross in the middle. Jesus was crucified between two men. On either side of the cross in "come," there is a character for the word "man." Can you see the characters?

Man

Come

Mrs. Lawson

Mrs. Lawson, a 73-year-old missionary widow from Scotland, was looking for a young woman to help her in China. Gladys heard about Mrs. Lawson at a prayer meeting and wrote a letter to her offering to help. Weeks later, Gladys received a reply that if she could reach China on her own, she could work with Mrs. Lawson. Mrs. Lawson and Gladys opened an inn called the Inn of Eight Happinesses. A few months after Gladys' arrival, Mrs. Lawson fell from a second-story balcony. She passed away not long after her fall.

Write "God Loves You"

The Chinese characters in the boxes to the right represent "shen ai nee", or "God loves you."

"Shen" (God) is written in nine steps.

"Ai" (love) is written in 11 steps.

"Nee" (you) is written in seven steps.

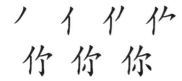

You can practice writing each character in the columns below the example.

Many of China's children have never heard

In fact, in China's schools, children are taught that there is no

Pray that God will provide ways for them to hear the Good News!

Gladys led the group on a 100-mile trek across the mountains.

Gladys and Mrs. Lawson welcomed muleteers to their Inn of Eight Happinesses. (A muleteer is a driver of a mule train. Mule trains carried goods from place to place, like big trucks do today.) The muleteers wanted to be entertained during their stay at the inn, so the women provided entertainment in the form of stories. The men had never heard the stories of a man named Jesus who "went about doing good" (Acts 10:38). Yang, the cook at the inn, helped Gladys learn Chinese words to tell the stories.

Missionaries and translators often introduce people to the Bible and the good news of Jesus by sharing Bible stories. They may begin with stories in Chapters 4 and 5 of the Gospel of Mark. Or they might tell some of the parables of Jesus, such as the Prodigal Son (Luke 15), the Good Samaritan (Luke 10), or the Lost Sheep (Matthew 18). Sometimes they first share stories from the Old Testament.

To Do

Choose a Bible story to learn well enough to present it to others. Read the story in a Bible or Bible storybook several times until you can tell it without looking at the book. Ask your parent or teacher if you can tell your family or class the story during a meal or other break. Share the story. If there is time, ask your listeners questions about it to learn what they remember and understand.

Here are some story suggestions:

A story from Mark 4–5 or a parable of Jesus

Daniel and the lion's den (Daniel 6)

David and Goliath (1 Samuel 17)

Jonah (the Book of Jonah)

Jeremiah's rescue (Jeremiah 38:1–13)

Jesus' birth (Luke 2:1–20)

Jesus' resurrection (Luke 24)

Moses and the burning bush (Exodus 3:1 – 4:17)

Noah (Genesis 6:9 – 9:17)

The Story of Creation (Genesis 1:1 – 2:4)

Fitting In

As a girl in England, Gladys Aylward sometimes felt like she didn't fit in. Gladys was less than five feet tall with black hair. Many other girls were blonde and much taller. But in China, the people were shorter and had black hair!

Is it ever a good thing not to fit in? If so, can you give some examples? If Gladys had fit in better in England, might it have been harder for her to leave her country and move to China?

_____

_____

When Gladys arrived in China, she gave up English customs to fit in with the people of China. Mrs. Smith, a missionary in China, gave Gladys clothes like those worn by Chinese women. In later years, Gladys said, "I lived exactly like a Chinese woman. I wore Chinese clothes, ate their food, spoke their language."

In other ways, Gladys did not try to fit in. One day she saw a woman trying to sell a little girl. It was a shocking sight! She reported the situation to the Mandarin — a government official. He told her to ignore it. Gladys said, "Mandarin, I did not come to China only to observe your laws. I came for the love of Jesus, and I shall act on the principles of His teaching, no matter what you say."

Should Gladys have obeyed the Mandarin to fit in? What are some ways you should not change to fit in?

_____

_____

Gladys began rescuing homeless children and caring for them, and the Mandarin began to respect her.

In what ways would you change to fit in with those around you if it would help you share the love of Christ better?

_____

_____

"Would you like to learn about Jesus?" a Christian girl asked a young man as she walked down the streets of her city. "Go away," the young man answered. The girl continued walking.

The young man was visiting the city. He knew very little about Jesus, and what he knew was not the truth. Later that day, an older man gave him a Christian tract and said, "This will teach you about eternal life with God!" The young man frowned as he grabbed the tract and threw it on the ground.

That night at a restaurant, a Christian couple approached the man and asked if he knew about Jesus and His love. "Three times in one day someone has tried to tell me about this Jesus," the young man thought. "He must be important."

He invited the couple to sit with him and listened as they told him how God sent Jesus to save the world from sin. In time, the young man became a follower of Jesus.

The first two Christians played a big part in opening the man's heart and mind to Jesus, but they probably never knew it. It must have been difficult to continue talking to people about Jesus after they were rejected, but they humbly obeyed God's command to tell others about Jesus.

If you had only one chance to talk to someone about Jesus, what would you tell them?

_____

_____

_____

To Think About

- Is someone in your town waiting for you to tell them about God's love?

- Are there people in other nations waiting for you to obey Jesus' command to pray that God will "send out laborers into his harvest" (Matthew 9:38)?

- Pray that God will lead you in your life and your prayers to those who are waiting to hear the Good News of Jesus' love!

A Man of LOVE

Richard's Story

"Russian communist officials invited thousands of religious leaders to a meeting in the Parliament building. Muslim mullahs, Jewish rabbis, and Christian pastors crowded into the great hall.

"My wife, Sabina, and I joined them. Top communists sat on a stage with a huge picture of Joseph Stalin behind them.

"The audience applauded the communists' statements, which were broadcast to the whole nation by radio. 'We want to be friends with church leaders!' the communists claimed. The crowd cheered. One pastor got up and said, 'You can count on us!' Another Christian said, 'Christianity and communism have a lot in common. Both believe in bringing about justice. We can work together!'

"One leader after another rose to give their comments in support of the Russians. Sabina couldn't stand it any longer. 'Richard,' she said, 'please stand up and wash away this shame from the face of Christ. They are spitting in His face.'

"'If I stand up for Christ, you will lose your husband,' I answered.

"'I don't need a husband who is a coward,' she said. I raised my hand to speak.

"'It is our duty to glorify God and Christ,' I said when I reached the microphone. 'We must first be loyal to Christ, not to earthly leaders. He is the one who died for us on the cross.'

"The people in the crowd seemed to suddenly wake up. A few began to clap. Many began to cheer, 'Pastor! Pastor!'

"'Your right to speak is withdrawn!' shouted a communist leader. 'Cut the microphone!' But the crowd cheered so loudly no one could hear him. Finally the wires to the microphone were cut. The shouting and clapping continued. Sabina and I made our way out of the hall through the noise and confusion. 'I have a powerful Savior. He'll do what is best for me,' I said.

"Later, the communists made me suffer for what I did at the meeting, but it was worth it."

Key Bible Verses:

"But I say to you who hear, Love your enemies, do good to those who hate you, bless those who curse you, pray for those who abuse [mock, insult, dishonor] you."
(Luke 6:27-28)

Key Word: LOVE

Love: An unselfish attitude of goodwill and concern for the good of others

In the 1940s, German Nazis occupied Romania. Many Christians were arrested. Richard was arrested and questioned three times, just because he was a pastor. After World War II ended, Russian communists took over Romania. Life under communism with the Russians was even more difficult than life under the Nazis had been.

✓ **Jewish Atheist**
Richard was born in Romania on March 24, 1909. He was the youngest of four boys. Though he was of Jewish descent, he grew up as an atheist, and he did not become a Christian until he was almost 30 years old.

✓ **Encountered by Jesus**
Richard became a Christian through the prayers of an elderly man located in a remote mountain village who had asked God to let him lead a Jew to Christ. Sabina put her trust in Jesus after Richard came to know Christ.

✓ **Messenger**
Richard was fluent in nine languages and wrote 18 books. His most well known book, *Tortured for Christ*, has been translated into 60 languages, with more than 3 million copies in print.

✓ **Prison Sermons**
While in prison, Richard composed sermons, which he committed to memory, and then preached in his cell. After his release, he wrote down the 350 sermons he was able to remember.

✓ **Imprisonment**
After being released in 1956, a pastor friend betrayed Richard to the authorities. Richard was arrested again in 1959, and released in 1964. He spent a total of 14 years in prison. His wife, Sabina, endured three harsh years in a prison labor camp.

✓ **Ransom**
Christians from Norway paid a $10,000 ransom for Richard's release, though the going rate for political prisoners was $1,900.

✓ **National Recognition**
Richard was named one of the ten most influential people of Romania.

✓ **Finishing the Race**
Sabina went to be with the Lord Aug. 11, 2000, at the age of 87. Richard followed on Feb. 17, 2001. He was 91 years old.

Morse Code Quote

While he was in prison, Richard Wurmbrand used a system based on Morse code to communicate with and witness to prisoners in other cells. The prisoners tapped messages on the walls between their cells.

Using the Morse code alphabet shown in the blue box, decode this quote from Richard Wurmbrand. Write each letter above the corresponding codes below to reveal the message.

The answer is in the Answer Key.

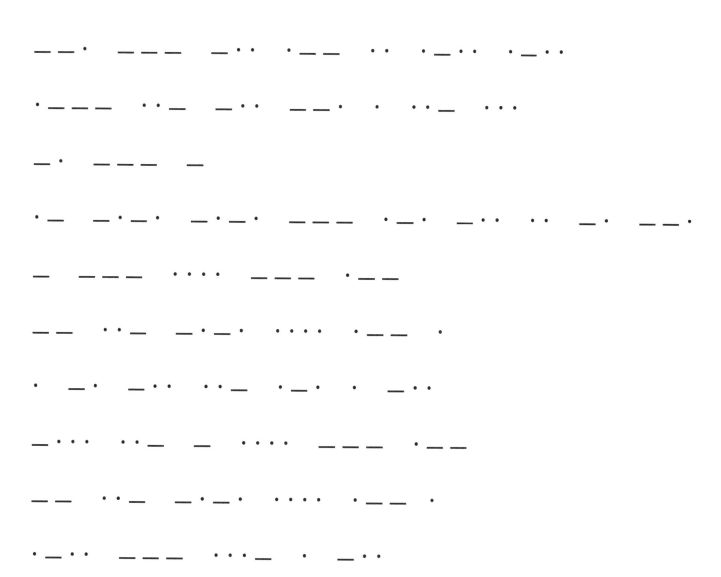

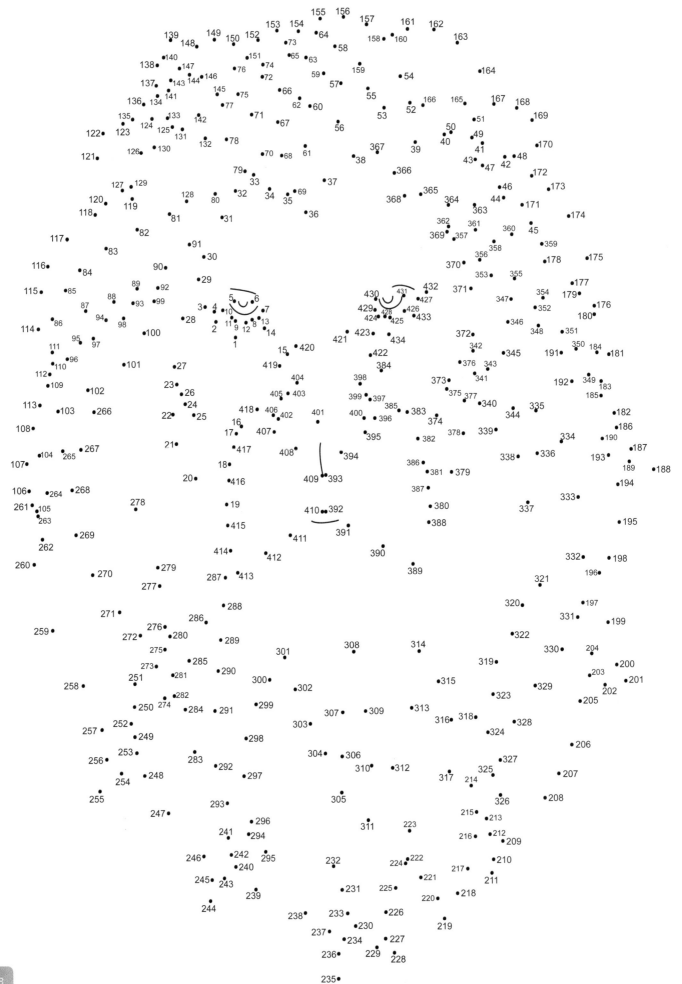

Before leaving Romania, Richard took a group of students to the zoo and stopped in front of the lions' cage. God rescued Daniel from the lions, Richard explained, but Daniel was ready to face the lions rather than deny God — without knowing whether or not he would be delivered. Early Christians also faced lions after they refused to deny Christ. Some died, standing firm in the Lord and loving those who tried to separate them from the love of God. "Our faith has not always been easy," Richard told the students.

After the Wurmbrands were imprisoned, generous Christians helped take care of Richard and Sabina's son, Mihai. But it was very risky to help the families of imprisoned Christians. One woman traveled many miles facing great difficulty to bring him a sack of potatoes — all she had to offer. The police discovered her kindness, took her to the police station, questioned her, and treated her harshly, simply for feeding a child.

Food was scarce in Romania during Richard Wurmbrand's time in prison, both inside and outside of prison. Sometimes people outside of prison ate the same simple food three times a day. In prison, they had much less.

Try This

Richard Wurmbrand often said that the prison guards ate the potatoes and the prisoners only had the peels made into a soup. Make your own "potato peel soup" by peeling a potato and then putting the peels (only) into a saucepan. **Add two cups of water. Bring the water to a boil for 5 minutes, then lower the heat and simmer for 10 minutes.** Let the "soup" cool, and then taste some. Romanian prisoners were thankful for even a potato peel meal!

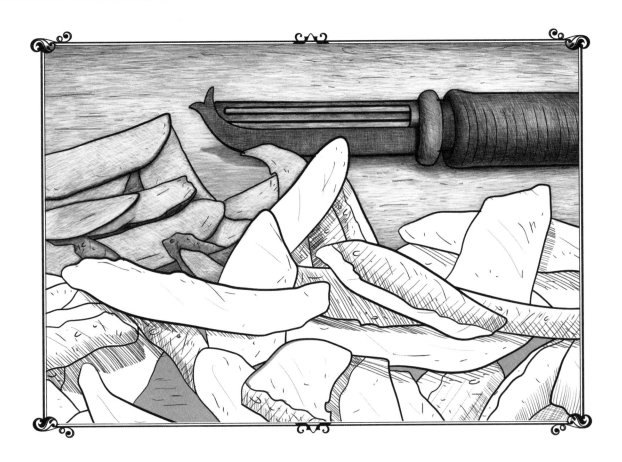

Richard's love for his betrayer

Richard helped out a younger pastor in his underground (secret) congregation, but later the man betrayed him by reporting Richard to the authorities. Richard was sent to prison. He had already been in prison for eight years, so he knew how hard it would be. On his way to prison, he asked Sabina to give his love to their son and to the pastor who betrayed him.

What would you do?

During his first imprisonment, Richard had suffered from serious illness, lack of food and medicine, beatings from the guards, solitary confinement for years, boredom, poor clothing and shoes, loneliness for his family, unheated cells, and many other miseries.

If you were in his place, how do you think you might feel toward the person who betrayed you, causing you to return to prison? What was Richard's reaction toward his betrayer?

_____

_____

> **Romans 12:17**
>
> "Repay no one evil for evil, but give thought to do what is honorable in the sight of all."

> A man in Richard's prison refused to betray even enemies who had mistreated him. Because the man refused to help them, the prison officials withheld medication from him that could have saved his life. He died in Richard's arms while giving glory to God.

A Christian prisoner's love

Romania's communist officials often did not trust each other. Sometimes they sent their own workers to prison. Sometimes the communist prisoners ended up in cells with Christians they had mistreated in the past. "I have seen Christians give away their last slice of bread (we were given one slice a week) and the medicine that would save their lives to a sick communist torturer who was now a fellow prisoner," Richard said.

What would you do?

If you had been in the prison with Christians and their former persecutors, do you think you would you have advised the Christians to give up their food and medicine to their enemies? Or would you have told them to keep the food and medicine for themselves?

_____

_____

Note: If someone mistreats you, tell your parents or a trusted adult.

Richard Wurmbrand knew that the Bible says, "Love your enemies" (Luke 6:27). How did Richard love his enemies?

- He forgave them when they wronged him, even those who betrayed and persecuted him.

- He told them how to repent of their sins and follow Christ. Richard said, "Many officers of the secret police to whom we witnessed became Christians and were happy to suffer in prison for having found our Christ. ... Only love can change the communist and the terrorist."

- He prayed for them. "In prison, I started every day with prayer," he said. "In my prayers, I traveled through the whole world, praying for every country and town I could remember. I prayed for pilots, sea captains, and those in prison. Then I prayed for my family, my friends, and my persecutors."

Enemies could take away Richard's freedom, his comfort, his health, and his Bible, and they could threaten to take away his life. But they couldn't take away his faith and his willingness to pray for them.

"Bless those who curse you, pray for those who mistreat you." (Luke 6:28, NIV)

Is there any way that a bad situation or an unkind person can stop you from praying?

_____

_____

_____

Is there something or someone that is troubling you or someone you love? Can you name anyone you need to forgive? Write a prayer for that person.

_____

_____

_____

A Woman of COURAGE

Perpetua's Story

The emperor, Severus, had decreed that no one could convert to Christianity. Roman soldiers raided Christian meetings and arrested people who were preparing for baptism. Perpetua was among those arrested. She was thrown into a gloomy Roman prison in the city of Carthage.

We know something about Perpetua's faith, life, zeal, and courage from the diary she kept during her imprisonment and from writings of other early Christians. She came from a wealthy Roman family and was well educated. She was married and had a baby boy. Prison officials did not allow Perpetua to be with her baby in the prison at first. But later they moved her to a more comfortable part of the prison, and her son stayed with her. "My prison has become a palace!" Perpetua wrote in her diary.

Perpetua's friend, Felicity, was also among the Christians who were arrested. Felicity, a slave, had trusted in Christ as her Savior. Now that both women were Christians, Perpetua no longer saw Felicity as a slave but as a beloved sister in Christ.

"Perform the sacrifice!" Perpetua's father begged when he visited her in prison. "Offer the sacrifice for the welfare of the emperor!" a Roman official ordered Perpetua at a court hearing. "I will not," she replied. The officials pronounced Perpetua and her friends guilty. "We returned to prison in high spirits," Perpetua wrote.

The Christians' courage and faith served as a witness for Christ to prison guards and officials. The believers also spoke to crowds that gathered near the prison, teaching them about God's coming judgment. "Thus everyone would depart from the prison in amazement, and many of them began to believe," wrote a Christian friend who added comments to Perpetua's diary.

Key Bible Verse:

"Have I not commanded you? Be strong and courageous. Do not be frightened, and do not be dismayed, for the Lord your God is with you wherever you go." (Joshua 1:9)

Key Word: COURAGE

Courage: Bravery in facing danger, fear, and difficulties.

Read Acts 5:40-42

How is the story in Acts similar to the account of Perpetua and her friends?

✓ **Dido**

According to ancient legends, a queen named Dido founded the North African city of Carthage where Perpetua lived. Today Carthage is a suburb of Tunis, Tunisia.

✓ **Punic Wars**

Carthage fought three wars against Rome called the Punic Wars. The Romans then became the rulers of Carthage.

✓ **Roman Empire**

In Perpetua's time, the Roman Empire controlled over 2.5 million square miles of land. The enormous amount of territory meant the need for control was also great, causing the leaders to become wary of threats to the security of the empire. Some officials considered Christians a threat. Roman officials accepted gods of other religions, but they expected Christians to honor Roman gods (and the emperor), along with their God.

✓ **Tertullian**

Tertullian, a Christian writer and church leader from Carthage, lived during the time Perpetua and her friends were in prison. He explained Christian beliefs to both Christians and non-Christians.

✓ **Saturus**

Saturus voluntarily joined Perpetua and her friends in prison. He is believed to have been their Christian teacher. Saturus and Perpetua both experienced visions while imprisoned. In Saturus' vision, he and Perpetua were carried to heaven where they joined those who had been martyred. In what ways would this vision encourage the prisoners?

✓ **The Ixthus**

"Ixthus" is the Greek word for fish. During the early days of Christianity, Christians were often put to death for practicing their faith, so, like persecuted Christians today, they worshiped in secret places. A fish painted on the outside door of a house let other Christians know that they would be safe and welcome inside.

I : Jesus
X: Christ
O: Son
Y: God
C: Savior

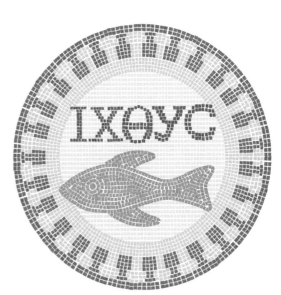

Can you find the 16 hidden crosses in the coloring page? The answer is in the Answer Key. Roman amphitheaters, like the one in the picture, were the scene of the many Christians' deaths.

God provided Perpetua with encouragement through fellow Christian prisoners.

Stained glass window of Perpetua and her friends

Perpetua's journal (diary) was one of the first known writings by a Christian woman. The journal describes Perpetua's sadness, joy, thankfulness, and encouragement in prison.

Journals can be used to describe events in your life, express your prayers to God, capture significant life lessons, or record spiritual events and milestones in your journey with God. Follow the instructions to make your own journal.

Needed: A hardback composition book and contact paper.

1. Open the book and lay it flat, cover side down, then measure it. Cut a piece of contact paper 2 inches larger than the book on all sides.

2. Center the open book on the piece of contact paper with the printed side of the paper down.

3. Cut the corners of the contact paper and the section next to the spine as shown in the picture.

4. Peel off about half of the backing on the contact paper and place the back of the composition book on the sticky paper, with the cut corners aligned with the corners of the book. Firmly press this half into place, folding the edges onto the inside of the back cover. Close the journal. Now peel off the rest of the protective paper and stick firmly to the front cover, folding the edges onto the inside of the front cover.

5. Feel free to decorate the cover of your journal or make reduced-sized photocopies of completed coloring pages from this activity book, and glue them to the cover or inside pages.

Perpetua and fellow believers bravely refused to participate in rituals that honored the emperor as if he were a god. A few decades after their death, a stricter emperor passed even harsher laws against Christians who refused to sacrifice to false gods.

Sometimes Christians who did not have the courage to oppose the emperor found ways to keep themselves out of trouble with Roman authorities. Anyone who sacrificed received a certificate stating that they had obeyed the law, so some paid their servants to go in their place and bring them back a certificate. Others would bribe an official to get the certificate.

What do you think?

Was it okay for some Christians to pretend to sacrifice to false gods in order to stay out of prison and continue taking care of their families? Why or why not? Write your thoughts on the lines below.

_____

_____

Read Matthew 10:32. Could Perpetua and her friends have offered a small sacrifice to get out of prison and still believe in Jesus in their hearts?

_____

_____

Perpetua's witness and courage brought many to Christ. Her story continues to challenge believers today to give themselves more fully to Him. If they had sacrificed, do you think others might have said, "Perpetua sacrificed to false gods and she's still a Christian, so maybe I can do the same?" the Apostle Paul said, "Give no offense [or cause to stumble] to Jews or to Greeks, or to the church of God" (1 Corinthians 10:32).

What do you think?

What do you think that means? How might it apply to the early Christians and sacrificing to false gods? Are there ways that Christians today can cause others to "stumble" by their actions (for example, doing sloppy work, repeating rude jokes, watching certain movies, or playing certain games)?

_____

_____

Onesimus was a runaway slave. In those days, slaves who ran away from their masters could be punished severely. The Apostle Paul had led both Onesimus and his master, Philemon, to Christ. After Onesimus ran away, Paul urged Philemon to forgive him instead of punishing him and to accept him "no longer as a slave, but better than a slave, as a dear brother."
(See Philemon 1:15–16, NIV.)

It might be hard to imagine slaves and their masters becoming friends and brothers in Christ. But Paul reminded Christians that, "there is no ... slave or free, but Christ is all, and is in all." (Colossians 3:11, NIV.)

Probably less than 200 years after Paul wrote those words, Perpetua and her slave, Felicity, became sisters in Christ and close friends. They were imprisoned together and suffered together for their faith. As Christians, they put Christ above everything else in their lives. It didn't matter that Perpetua was wealthy, and Felicity was a slave.

Choose a Friend, Be a Friend

When you go to a new school, church, or activity, do you make friends with people who seem to be most like you on the outside? Do you consider any of the following when you choose a new friend?

- Can I talk to the person about God, the Bible, and my faith?

- Does the person complain about parents, rules, and school, or would their behavior be a good example for me? Would I be a good example for them?

- Is the person kind to people who need help? Could I be helpful to the person?

- Would I enjoy working on tasks or goals with the person, or do they look for ways to avoid responsibilities? Am I easy to work with?

- Would we be concerned about each other's needs? Philippians 2:3 says, "Do nothing out of selfish ambition or vain conceit. Rather, in humility value others above yourselves" (NIV).

As friends, Perpetua and Felicity gave each other courage in their walk with God, helped each other in times of trouble, and inspired each other to greater love for the Lord.

Proverbs 12:26
"The righteous choose their friends carefully, but the way of the wicked leads them astray" (NIV).

A Woman of KINDNESS

Amy's Story

"I have feelings of fear about the future," said Amy Carmichael. Amy, who grew up in Northern Ireland, was a new missionary serving the Lord in Japan. She was concerned that she didn't know where God would lead her next.

She visited a cave in the mountains to be alone with God and to pray about her future. Would she ever get married? Would she have any children? If she continued serving the Lord alone, would she get lonely? Amy felt the Lord saying to her, "None of them that trust in Me shall be desolate." ("Desolate" means abandoned, forsaken, or alone.) The reassurance from God stayed with Amy throughout her life.

Amy returned to the mission field — this time in India — where she gathered a small group of Christian women to help her witness among the people. The women called themselves "the Starry Cluster." They hoped to "shine like the ... stars forever and ever" and to "lead many to righteousness" (Daniel 12:3, NIV).

> **Key Bible Verse:**
>
> "Put on then, as God's chosen ones, holy and beloved, compassionate hearts, kindness, humility, meekness, and patience." (Colossians 3:12)

> **Key Word: KINDNESS**
>
> Kindness: The quality of being friendly, thoughtful, helpful, and willing to share

Amy's ministry is most remembered for rescuing "temple girls." Some Hindu families offered their daughters to Hindu temples to work as servants. They believed that their gift would please the gods and bring them good fortune.

Battling many obstacles, Amy and her co-workers for the Lord rescued dozens of temple children. Some grew up to continue Amy's ministry, thankful for God's grace and the missionaries' kindness. Instead of experiencing the loneliness she had feared when she was younger, Amy became the mother of many children whose lives she had saved.

About 30 years after Amy began saving the children, she fell and injured her leg. The injury kept her bedridden for the next 20 years. Amy continued to serve God by writing numerous books and thousands of letters from her bed. She died in India at the age of 83.

✓ **"If Only You Knew"**
Amy Carmichael grew up in a well-to-do Irish family with six younger siblings. She often got in trouble for her behavior. Once when someone told her she was naughty, she thought to herself, "If only you knew how much naughtier I could be, you wouldn't think I was naughty at all!"

✓ **Serving God at Home**
As a teenager, Amy totally gave her life and future to God. Her father died when she was 18, and Amy spent the next 10 years helping care for her younger siblings.

✓ **Learning Kindness**
One day after church, Amy and her brother saw an old beggar woman with torn clothes and only rags to cover her feet. They helped the woman, but Amy was embarrassed to be seen with the pitiful beggar. Then the Lord reminded her of the things that would be important in eternity. (Read 1 Corinthians 3:12-14.) She was no longer embarrassed, and she promised God to do things that pleased Him.

✓ **No Furloughs**
Most missionaries take furloughs — breaks to rest and return to their home country and families — but Amy served in India for 55 years without a furlough.

✓ **Castes**
Traditional Hinduism teaches that people are born into castes. A caste is a social class. Priests belong to the highest caste, soldiers to the next, businessmen and farmers to the next, and servants and workers to the next. Lowest of all are the "untouchables," now called Dalits. As a foreigner, Amy would have been seen as an "untouchable." Today the government of India has laws against the caste system. But Dalits are still scorned in parts of India.

✓ **Amy's Prayer**
The morning before the accident that broke her leg and made her an invalid, Amy prayed, "Do with me as Thou wilt. Do anything that will fit me to serve Thee and help my beloveds." During this time, Amy wrote many books and thousands of letters encouraging believers to take up their cross and follow Jesus.

Complete the dot to dot to reveal one of the world's best known landmarks in India. The Taj Mahal was built in the 1600s by order of the emperor in memory of his wife, who died at the age of 38 after giving birth to their 14th child. The Taj Mahal serves as a burial place for the emperor and his wife.

Amy rescued children from their lives as temple slaves.

Kindness Rocks

Has someone ever been kind to you without finding out how their kindness helped you? Can you show kindness without expecting anything in return?

You can make kindness rocks to bless others, but often you will not be there when they enjoy your gift. But you can thank God for the opportunity to encourage others!

- Gather rocks about 3 to 5 inches wide. At least one side of the rocks should be flat and smooth. Following the directions on the paint can, spray the rocks with any color of acrylic spray paint. Let the rocks dry thoroughly.

- Draw a picture or write a message on each rock, using fine-point oil-based paint pens. Let the paint dry.

- Seal the rocks with clear acrylic coating spray. Let the spray dry.

- Place the rocks in a park or leave them on a beach or in another place for others to find.

Amy Carmichael's kindness brought joy and hope to many children and adults in India. "Miss Carmichael was a blessing to all who came into ... contact with her radiant life," said a missionary friend of Amy.

Who Has a Need?

Amy Carmichael noticed the needs of those around her and tried to meet those needs when she could. For one week, keep a record of people who have a need. They can be people you know, people someone tells you about, or people in the news in your town or elsewhere. Put the names of the people under their specific needs on the chart below. You can put a name in more than one column.

Pray: Are there people who don't yet know Jesus that you can pray for? Have you heard about people in a place where a disaster occurred? Will you ask God to heal someone? Will you ask God to lead you to someone He wants you to bless?

Encourage: Is there someone in your town who publicly stands up for the truth? Can you send a message of encouragement to that person or to those in your community who work hard to serve others? Will you thank the "invisible" servants in your family or church who keep things running smoothly? Could you send cards or notes to family or friends who are sick or to the family members of someone who has died?

Help: Can you volunteer to help in your church or participate in a community service project? Can you run an errand or do a chore for a neighbor? Can you do a project to raise funds for a sick child or a family whose house was destroyed by fire, flood, tornado, or hurricane?

Find Help: If you see a homeless person with no coat, can you find a ministry that helps homeless people and tell them about the need or offer to donate a coat? If you know a student at school who has a need, will you talk with your parents to determine the right way to help them?

Fill in the chart below with people who could use prayer, encouragement, or help. Pick one or more people from your chart each week, ask the Lord to inspire you, and bless them with His kindness.

Pray	Courage	Help

The Blessings of Kindness

Amy Carmichael was called to share Jesus' love with the people of India — that was her mission. While she was sharing the gospel, she came upon suffering children who needed her help.

But why should we be kind and helpful to others? We cannot earn salvation for ourselves or others by our good deeds.

- **We Follow Jesus' Example**
  God sent Jesus into the world "that whoever believes in him should not perish but have eternal life" (John 3:16). That was Jesus' mission. But He also fed the hungry, healed the sick, washed His disciples' feet, blessed children, and much more. He told His followers to do the same.

- **We Follow What the Bible Says**
  Luke 6:35, tells us to do good to our enemies because God is kind to even the ungrateful and evil, as well as those who obey Him. First Corinthians 13 says, "Love is patient and kind." Ephesians 4 instructs Christians to be kind and forgiving, and Galatians 5 lists kindness as a fruit of the Spirit.

> **We trust in God's good plans for our lives**

Amy was well prepared to care for children, as she had taken care of her six younger siblings. But she thought she might never be a mother. She never dreamed that she would help dozens of temple children. The children were a blessing to her.

Proverbs 11:17 says,
"A man who is kind benefits himself."

How did Amy's kindness benefit her? Have you ever helped someone and been blessed in some way as a result?

_____

_____

When you help someone, what are your reasons for doing so?

_____

_____

A Man of OBEDIENCE

William's Story

London's Great Exhibition of 1851 drew people from all over the world. Visitors were amazed by new inventions, many of which had brought better jobs and living conditions to everyone in England — except the very poorest people. Their lives seemed to get steadily worse. Some gave up trying to live righteously and began abusing alcohol. As a result, many fell into immoral living.

William Booth, a preacher in England, had given his life to Christ as a teenager. He wanted to obey God, no matter where God called him. As it turned out, God called William and his wife, Catherine, to the East End of London where people lived in great poverty with little hope.

William and Catherine began preaching to the poor people in the East End, setting up soup kitchens to serve daily meals and provide other services to help the people live more hopeful lives. But their obedience was not always easy. Not everyone was happy about the help. Bar owners lost money when people stopped getting drunk and started following the Lord.

But sometimes help came from unexpected places. Peter Monk, an Irish prizefighter, attended a meeting where William was preaching. Even though Peter enjoyed fighting and was not a Christian, he didn't like it when a rowdy crowd began to mock William and shout at him. He firmly calmed the crowd and soon became a follower of Jesus. People who didn't like William's ministry continued to threaten and oppose him and his helpers.

After one year, the Booths had 60 new Christians helping them reach people for Christ. They called their ministry "The Christian Mission." William believed they were fighting a war against sin. They began to use military terms, referring to William as "General." After a time, they changed their name to the Salvation Army, wore uniforms, and created their own flag, symbols, and music. Their "sword" was the Bible, and their magazine was called *The War Cry*.

Today, the ministry the Booths started helps people in more than 120 countries, sharing Jesus' love while providing health care, education, and disaster relief.

Key Bible Verse:

"Observe the commands of the Lord your God, walking in obedience to him and revering him."
(Deuteronomy 8:6, NIV)

Key Word: OBEDIENCE

Obedience: The willingness to serve or please another, or to carry out their commands or instructions; dutiful

✓ William and Catherine's Childhood

William had learned something about poverty while he was growing up. He had to quit school and go to work at age 13 to help support his family. Catherine did not have an easy childhood either. A spinal condition kept her in bed for months at a time. But she was able to read the entire Bible eight times before she was 12!

✓ Red Kettles

In 1891, a Salvation Army officer in San Francisco noticed that many poor people were hungry, and he decided to provide a Christmas dinner for as many needy people as he could. He placed a kettle in a public place to collect money for his project. Every year at Christmastime, the Salvation Army still collects donations in red kettles to help them meet the needs of the poor.

✓ Salvation Army Bands

Salvation Army bands helped calm disruptive crowds. The musicians borrowed tunes from popular songs of the day and added Christian words. At first, William was not sure that it was a good idea to allow the bands at Salvation Army events. But he grew to appreciate them. Today Salvation Army music programs teach children to sing and play instruments to glorify God and bless those who hear them.

✓ Last Respects

The Booths became very well known for their work. Catherine, the "Mother of the Salvation Army," died in 1890, and more than 30,000 people attended her funeral. When William died in 1912, the Salvation Army announced, "The general has laid down his sword." Tens of thousands also attended his funeral, and he was mourned by monarchs, heads of state, the wealthy and poor alike.

As a teenager, William Booth surrendered his life and future in obedience to God. Unscramble the words in the sentence below to see what he said.

ODG HSLLA EVHA LLA HTREE SI FO IWLLIAM OTBOH.

_____

After William became a preacher, God led him to minister among the poorest of the poor of London. Unscramble the words in the following sentence to find out what William said about preaching to the poor.

UOY ONACNT WMRA ETH RASTHE FO OPPEEL IHWT GDO'S

ELVO FI YHTE HEAV NA PMEYT STOMAHC NAD DOLC TFEE.

_____

_____

Read James 2:15–16. How do the verses agree with what William said?

William encouraged others to follow God's will for their lives. Unscramble the words in the following sentence to find out what he told Christians about how to discover the will of God.

LEEVIBE WHTI LAL RYOU MIHGT LAL EH AHS IASD NI HSI YHOL DROW.

_____

_____

Answers are in the Answer Key.

William Booth preaching

Tasty Encouragement

National Donut Day is celebrated on the first Friday in June every year. Some donut shops offer free donuts in honor of the day.

But donut companies didn't start the event. The Salvation Army created the celebration in 1938. The first Donut Day raised funds for poor people. Since then, the Salvation Army has observed the day in honor of Salvation Army women who made donuts for American soldiers in France during World War I. Salvation Army workers again served donuts to soldiers during World War II and the Vietnam War.

Today, following the example of William Booth, the Salvation Army serves millions of free meals — including donuts — every year to people in need.

Do you know someone you could encourage with a plate of donuts? You don't have to wait for National Donut Day! Try the recipe below if you want to share homemade donuts with someone who needs encouragement.

Donut Recipe
Ingredients:

1. Package of large canned biscuits

2. Peanut or vegetable oil

3. Icing or cinnamon sugar (optional)

- Use a 1-inch round cookie cutter or bottle lid to cut a hole in the center of each biscuit. Keep the dough you removed from the biscuit.

- In a large pot or deep fryer, heat about 2 inches of oil over medium to medium-high heat (about 350 degrees). (Make sure a grownup helps.)

- Fry the donuts and holes until they are golden brown on one side, then turn them over and cook the other side.

- Drain on paper towels. If desired, spread icing on them, or coat them in cinnamon sugar.

- Deliver to someone with a note or word of encouragement!

What Do You Think?

William Booth wanted to help Christian parents of his day raise children to serve the Lord obediently. Below are some of his instructions for parents.

God's Love

"The goodness and love of God should be explained to children very early in life ... that God is not only willing but anxious, for Christ's sake, to pardon their sins, and become at once, as a natural consequence, their Father and Friend." Do you agree that it is a good idea to teach these truths to very young children? Why or why not?

_____

_____

Keeping Silent

"Compel children to keep silence in the presence of grown-up people. Nevertheless, it will be good to give them every opportunity in their own play-time, or somewhere in the absence of strangers, to express their impressions about what they see and hear and learn. At such times converse with them freely; answer their questions." What do you think of William's rule?

_____

_____

Friends

"Prevent [children] from having association with their schoolmates. Let them mix as little as possible with them after school hours, going to and coming from the school alone, and keeping as much as possible by themselves in the playground." Do you agree with William's rules about classmates from school?

_____

_____

Putting Others First

"Teach your children to deny themselves in order to promote the happiness of others. Train them to give the preference to brothers and sisters in things that are most desirable. If there is a better seat at the table ... or in [church]; if there is nicer food, or a more desirable toy — teach them to let their brothers and sisters or friends have it." What do you think of William's suggestion about sharing the best things with others? Can you find any verses from the Bible to support William's suggestion?

_____

_____

William Booth saw horrifying sights when he visited London's East End. Homeless people slept outside, many families were sick and had no way to go to a doctor, and most were hungry and cold. William noted that horses in England got better care than the people of the East End.

Temptations to sin were everywhere. One visitor said that bars had little stair steps at the counter so even small children could reach the alcohol.

It seemed to William that no one outside the East End was paying attention to the people and problems there. He and Catherine championed (to support the cause of, defend) those who could not speak up for themselves. They spent the rest of their lives telling the needy people about Jesus and speaking and writing to others on their behalf.

- Are there situations in which you could speak up for others?

- Are there times when it is right to be silent and not speak up?

- If you are with a group of kids making fun of someone who is not present, is that a good time to speak up for the person who is not there?

- Has someone ever spoken up for you?

- Have you ever heard someone speak out against Christians who speak up for Christian beliefs? What is the best way to speak up for the truth and for other Christians?

> *"God loves with a great love the man whose heart is bursting with a passion for the impossible."*
>
> — **William Booth**

Sometimes it's not easy to speak up. Others may reject your efforts in the same way people opposed the Booths. You can receive courage and strength to obey from God, the Bible, your parents, and other Christians who are willing to join you in speaking up.

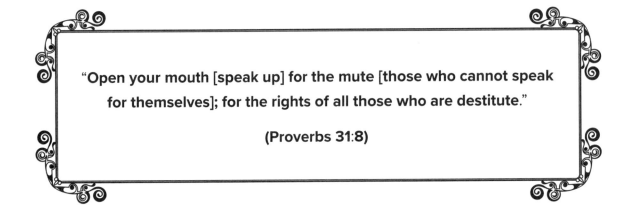

"Open your mouth [speak up] for the mute [those who cannot speak for themselves]; for the rights of all those who are destitute."

(Proverbs 31:8)

A Man of FAITHFULNESS

Samuel's Story

The situation looked hopeless. Warriors from an enemy tribe had tied Prince Kaboo to a pole and surrounded him. Kaboo's father, who ruled his tribe as chief, had been unable to rescue Kaboo after the enemies kidnapped him.

A scowling warrior raised his spear and aimed it straight at Kaboo. But then, a bright light flashed from the sky, and a voice said, "Run, Kaboo, run!" The ropes fell off and Kaboo ran into the jungle.

Kaboo found his way to a plantation where the owners allowed him to stay and work. He was also able to attend church services. One day at church, he heard the story of Saul on the road to Damascus from Acts 9.

Kaboo ran to the front of the church saying, "I know that voice!" He realized that his heavenly Father had rescued him, and he faithfully devoted the rest of his life to Him.

To testify of his new life, he changed his name to Samuel Morris after a Christian teacher he had heard about from an American missionary named Lizzie McNeil.

Samuel was happy with his new life, but he was sad that the African tribal people in his country of Liberia did not know about Jesus. He decided to go to America to learn to be a missionary like Lizzie.

> **Key Bible Verse:**
>
> "Only fear the Lord and serve him faithfully with all your heart. For consider what great things he has done for you."
> (1 Samuel 12:24)

> **Key Word: FAITHFULNESS**
>
> Faithfulness: The quality of being faithful, unchanging loyalty, devotion to the truth

> "He thought he was coming to prepare to be a missionary to the people of Africa, but it was to prepare Taylor [University] for its mission to the whole world!"
>
> — Taylor University President

Samuel made the grueling and dangerous voyage to America. The sailors fought storms, illness, exhausting work, and each other. Many of them bullied and threatened Samuel, but God prevailed. By the end of the voyage, many of the crew wanted to follow Samuel's God!

In America, Samuel shared and lived out his faith in New York and at Taylor University in Indiana.

Samuel died when he was only 20 years old. Though he never became a missionary to Africa, his faithfulness to God and his testimony inspired many to become missionaries and spread the Good News of Jesus all over the world.

New York City

Samuel arrived in New York City with his small bag and the intention of meeting with Stephen Merritt, a pastor and the director of a mission in the city. New York City was already a big place when Samuel arrived in 1891. The population was more than 1.5 million. Samuel had no idea where to find Mr. Merritt in the vast city, and the majority of people did not have telephones in the late 1800s. Amazingly, the first person Samuel asked knew the pastor and took him to meet him! Surely, God was guiding Samuel!

Taylor University

Mr. Merritt helped Samuel get accepted to Taylor University in Indiana. Humbly, Samuel said, "If there is a room [at Taylor] no one wants, I'll take it." While he was at Taylor, he spent a great deal of time praying, reading his Bible, and talking with others about Jesus. He prayed daily for an atheist student who later devoted his life to God and became a missionary.

Missionary to America

Samuel died when he was 20 years old. It seemed like he might have failed in his mission — he never became a missionary to Africa. But his faithfulness to God was such an inspiration to those whose lives he touched in America, that many who heard about him did become missionaries and spread the gospel all over the world.

Liberia

- **Algeria**
- **Democratic Republic of the Congo (DRC)**
- **Sudan**
- **Libya**
- **Chad**
- **Niger**
- **Angola**
- **Mali**
- **South Africa**
- **Ethiopia**
- **Mauritania**
- **Egypt**
- **Tanzania**
- **Nigeria**
- **Namibia**
- **Mozambique**
- **Zambia**
- **South Sudan**
- **Somalia**
- **Central African Republic (CAR)**
- **Madagascar**
- **Botswana**
- **Kenya**
- **Cameroon**
- **Morocco**

Listed above are the 25 largest African countries, ordered by size of landmass. Write the countries' names in the right location on the map. Look online or use an atlas if you need help. Samuel was from the African country of Liberia. Color the map when complete.

A light flashed from the sky and a voice said, "Run, Kaboo, run!"

African Witness Bracelet

Needed: Colorful strips of paper 1 inch wide and 8½ inches long (such as gift-wrap or construction paper); straws; tape; buttons or other colorful items that can be strung on a bracelet; and yarn, ribbon, fishing line, or leather cord

To make African "beads," place a straw on one end of a paper strip, perpendicular to the strip. Fold the end of the strip over the straw, and tape it to the strip. Roll up the straw in the paper to the other end of the strip. Tape the end shut, then gently pull the straw out.

Repeat with more strips. String the "beads" on yarn, ribbon, or fishing line.

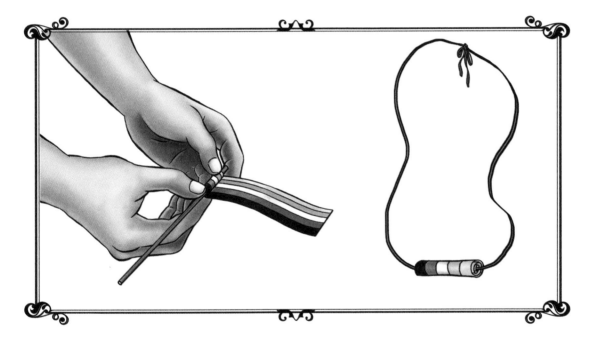

To make a "witness chain," make your beads black, red, white, green and gold. Black stands for sin, which is not allowed in heaven. Red symbolizes the blood that Jesus shed to save those who believe in Him so they can be with Him in heaven forever. White represents the clean heart of those who admit their sin to God, believe in His Son, Jesus, and call on Him to save them from their sin. Green is the color of growing things. Our relationship with God grows when we pray, read the Bible, gather with other believers for worship, and share the Good News of Jesus with others. Gold represents heaven, where God lives and everything is perfect.

Wear One and Share One

Make two beaded witness chains. Keep one for yourself, and give the other to someone else as you share God's plan of salvation with him or her.

Samuel told many people how God had saved him. A personal testimony is vital when witnessing to others. To prepare a testimony, complete the sentences and sections below. You might want to keep a copy of your answers in your Bible. Review and update it from time to time. Perhaps you can practice sharing it with a family member, classmate, or friend.

Before I became a Christian

_____

_____

When I became a Christian

_____

_____

How I heard about salvation by faith in Christ

_____

_____

Some of my favorite promises in the Bible are (Examples of biblical promises are Philippians 4:13, Psalm 27:1, Hebrews 4:16, and Matthew 6:33.)

_____

_____

God keeps His promises. One time when I experienced this was

_____

_____

Some of the things God has done for me in my life are (See 2 Corinthians 5:17.)

_____

_____

The best thing about following Jesus is

_____

_____

"But in your hearts honor Christ the Lord as holy, always being prepared to make a defense to anyone who asks you for a reason for the hope that is in you; yet do it with gentleness and respect" (1 Peter 3:15).

Samuel Morris was left waiting in an office while the man he came to see, Stephen Merritt, went to a meeting. Mr. Merritt was a pastor Samuel had heard about in Africa. Samuel went to the office at Mr. Merritt's mission in New York City when he first arrived in America. "I have come from Africa to learn from you about the Holy Spirit," Samuel told Mr. Merritt.

What do you do when you have to wait in a doctor's office or somewhere else? Do you read? Fidget? Pray? Play a game?

Samuel had to wait a long time because Mr. Merritt forgot about him after his meeting! Later that night, Mr. Merritt returned to his office. What do you suppose he found Samuel doing? Samuel was faithfully giving his testimony to the men at the mission. While Mr. Merritt was gone, Samuel had led 17 of the men to Christ!

Samuel stayed with Mr. Merritt for about a month. One Sunday, Mr. Merritt took Samuel to a youth Sunday school class. Samuel was different from the other students in many ways, and they laughed at him. But by the time Mr. Merritt came to get Samuel after the class, Samuel had shared his testimony with the group and they were weeping, sobbing, and repenting of their sins.

Can you think of some places where you regularly go and could tell someone about Jesus? Write them below.

_____

_____

A Man of TRUTHFULNESS

Augustine's Story

Augustine felt sick — "soul sick," he called it. For so long, he had searched for truth, and he was weary of the search. He tried to find it through study and education, various religious teachings, ambition, achievement, positions of power, possessions, and even immorality. Nothing relieved the emptiness in his heart or gave him peace.

Distressed and upset, Augustine ran into a garden one day. "I cast myself down, I know not how, under a fig tree, giving full vent to my tears," he later wrote in his book *Confessions*.

As he cried, his mother, Monica, was no doubt praying for him. She had cried and prayed for Augustine when he was a disobedient child, breaking rules and skipping school. As a youth, Augustine looked for pleasure in sinful activities, and his mother continued to cry and pray. Throughout his rebellious life, his mother had prayed and wept for his salvation and deliverance.

As Augustine wept, he heard a voice saying, "Take up and read, take up and read." He picked up part of the New Testament that he had been reading earlier that day. As he read Chapter 13 from the Book of Romans, he knew he had to give up living for himself and surrender to God. His search was over.

He knew the truth, and it would set him free from his distress and from his miserable life. After further study, he was baptized.

Less than a year after his baptism, his mother died, but not before he had a chance to visit her and tell her the good news of his conversion. "God has done this for me more abundantly, that I should see you now, giving up earthly pleasures and becoming his servant," Monica said.

Augustine later became a church leader in a city called Hippo. He spent the last 40 years of his life fighting false ideas and teachings that were leading people away from the truth. Augustine died in Hippo at the age of 75.

Key Bible Verse:

"And you will know the truth, and the truth will set you free." (John 8:32)

Key Word: TRUTHFULNESS

Truthfulness: The quality of telling the truth (the real facts about something)

Fascinating Facts!

Tagaste
Augustine was born on Nov. 13, A.D. 354, in Tagaste, which is located in a region that is now the country of Algeria. Today more than 95 percent of Algerians are Muslim.

Patricus
Augustine's father, Patricus, was a short-tempered man who opposed Christianity. Augustine was one of three children. Patricus trusted in Christ as his Savior on his deathbed in 371.

Adeodatus
In his youth, Augustine fathered a son by his girlfriend. His name was Adeodatus. Augustine later broke up with his girlfriend but remained close to his son. Sadly, Adeodatus died at age 16.

The Beggar
One day, before he came a Christian, Augustine passed by a laughing beggar. He was amazed by the beggar's happiness. "He has what I cannot attain to," Augustine thought. He later learned that joy does not come from earthly pleasures. Augustine reportedly died owning no personal possessions.

A Mother's Tears
After Monica had prayed and cried for years over her wayward son, she asked a Christian leader for help and advice. He told her, "It cannot be that the son of these tears should perish." Monica took comfort in his words. She believed Augustine would surrender his life to Christ before she died. And her faith was rewarded!

The City of God
In his book *The City of God*, Augustine described the errors in the thinking of people who don't follow Christ and the Bible. He explained that God is in control of history and that countries that do not honor God will not last forever.

Fighting Heresies
After Augustine became a Christian, he wanted to save others from the false ways of thinking that had ruled his life in the past. So he spoke and wrote against heresies. He wrote several books and more than 100 treatises. (Heresy is a belief or idea that does not agree with the accepted truth of Christianity. A treatise is a book or written material that discusses the facts and principles of a particular subject.)

Augustine's Words of Wisdom

Find the bolded words from Augustine's quotes below. The words can be found vertically, horizontally, and diagonally. Each word appears in the puzzle twice. Answers are in the Answer Key.

1. "You have made us for **Yourself**, O Lord, and our **hearts** are **restless** until they rest in You."

2. "What does love look like? It has the **hands** to help others. It has the feet to hasten to the poor and **needy**. It has eyes to see **misery** and want. It has the ears to hear the **sighs** and **sorrows** of men. That is what love looks like."

3. "God **loves** each of us as if there were **only** one of us."

4. "What **grace** is meant to do is to help good people, not to **escape** their **sufferings**, but to bear them with a stout heart, with a fortitude that finds its strength in **faith**."

5. "Faith is to believe what you do not yet see; the **reward** for this faith is to see what you believe."

6. "If you believe what you like in the **gospel** and **reject** what you don't like, it is not the gospel you believe, but yourself."

7. "The **Bible** was **composed** in such a way that as beginners mature, its meaning **grows** with them."

c	a	r	r	e	s	t	l	e	s	s	z	b	y	m	i	s	e	r	y
o	c	e	x	d	o	n	l	y	p	i	w	e	v	r	f	t	g	s	o
m	h	j	r	i	r	n	q	j	p	g	i	o	n	e	e	d	y	k	u
p	r	e	w	a	r	d	l	n	l	h	m	a	z	j	b	b	y	c	r
o	w	c	d	v	o	e	o	y	n	s	u	f	f	e	r	i	n	g	s
s	u	t	f	t	w	g	v	s	e	h	r	a	i	c	q	b	j	o	e
e	p	k	o	l	s	n	e	m	e	a	b	i	z	t	y	l	c	s	l
d	w	c	o	m	p	o	s	e	d	d	x	t	e	v	f	e	u	p	f
g	b	t	h	s	i	r	j	q	y	k	p	h	a	n	d	s	l	e	o
m	m	i	s	e	r	y	a	b	c	y	z	x	g	d	w	u	e	l	u
f	t	g	b	s	h	r	i	p	j	o	k	n	r	g	l	f	m	a	b
r	e	s	t	l	e	s	s	z	y	c	h	x	a	r	d	f	w	e	v
y	s	f	g	h	e	a	r	t	s	u	e	s	c	a	p	e	t	h	s
o	c	i	g	r	j	q	e	k	p	l	a	g	e	c	o	r	n	m	a
u	a	z	o	b	y	x	w	c	d	w	r	e	r	e	v	i	f	g	t
r	p	u	s	h	s	h	a	n	d	s	t	i	r	o	j	n	q	k	s
s	e	p	p	l	s	o	r	r	o	w	s	o	m	a	w	g	n	y	i
e	b	w	e	c	v	d	d	u	e	t	f	g	r	o	w	s	r	g	g
l	o	v	e	s	p	h	o	i	n	j	m	k	a	l	f	a	i	t	h
f	p	r	e	d	m	o	f	r	g	o	s	p	e	l	a	y	b	c	s

Augustine preaching

A voice said to Augustine, "Take up and read."

Make a Mosaic

Mosaics are pictures or designs made of small pieces of ceramic tile, glass, stone, or other materials. You can make a mosaic out of "gems."

Needed: White craft glue that dries "clear and durable," several small disposable containers such as yogurt containers, food coloring, a disposable spoon or craft stick, aluminum foil, and scissors.

Instructions :

1. Pour about 1 ounce (1/4 of a four-ounce bottle) of the glue into a small disposable container. Use a different container for each different color of gem you want to make.

2. Add 1 or 2 drops of food coloring to the glue and mix well with a plastic spoon or craft stick.

3. Drop small blobs of the colored glue 1 inch apart on a large sheet of aluminum foil. The blobs will spread out to form ovals or circles. If they spread out too flat, add more glue to the mixture. It will take several days for the gems to dry and become glassy.

4. Draw a mosaic design on a small piece of paper or cardstock. After they dry, cut the gems with scissors into shapes that will allow you to recreate your design. Set the gems on the paper or cardstock to form the mosaic. Hint: Start in the center of the paper and work outward, covering all parts of the paper without leaving spaces between the gems. Then glue the gems to the paper or cardstock in the pattern of your picture or design.

What Do You Think?

Augustine spent many years speaking and writing against the false ideas of his day.

Before he became a Christian, Augustine belonged to a group which taught that, "knowledge is the only way to salvation." Using one or more of the Bible verses at the bottom of this page (or another verse you know), tell why that belief does not agree with Christian teachings. Write your thoughts on the lines below.

_____

_____

False ideas are also accepted by some people today. Can you refute the ideas below using a verse in the list at the bottom of the page or other verses? (Refute: To explain why something is false.)

False Ideas:

• All religions are just opinions, so they cannot be right or wrong. People do not need to believe in one particular path to find salvation or the truth.

• What do you think? What does the Bible say?

_____

_____

• After someone dies, their soul is born again and again until it becomes part of the universe. This belief is called reincarnation.

• What do you think? What does the Bible say?

_____

_____

To Consider:

• "He died for us so that, whether we are awake or asleep, we may live together with him." (1 Thessalonians 5:10, NIV)

• "Jesus said to him, 'I am the way, and the truth, and the life. No one comes to the Father except through me.'" (John 14:6)

• "I am the door. If anyone enters by me, he will be saved and will go in and out and find pasture." (John 10:9)

Ahab was a wicked king of Israel. Jehoshaphat, the king of Judah, did right in God's eyes. One day, the two kings talked together. "Will you go with me to fight at Ramoth-gilead?" Ahab asked.

Jehoshaphat agreed to go with Ahab. "But first," he said, "we should ask for God's guidance." So Ahab called together about 400 of his ungodly prophets. "Go fight the battle," they told Ahab. "You will win."

But Jehoshaphat wanted to hear from a true man of God. "There is still one man like that," Ahab said. "But I hate him. He never says anything good about me, only bad."

"You shouldn't talk like that!" Jehoshaphat said.

Ahab sent for Micaiah, a true prophet of God. Even though Micaiah was pressured to say what the king wanted to hear, he had to speak the truth. "Whatever the Lord says to me, that I will speak," said Micaiah. "You will lose if you go to battle," he told Ahab. Micaiah told Ahab that his 400 prophets were not telling the truth. Then the king sent him to prison. While he was in prison, the kings went to battle. Ahab was killed, and his army lost, just as Micaiah had said.

(This story is found in 1 Kings 22.)

To Talk About

- How do you think Micaiah felt when he was the only one telling God's truth?

- How does standing up for the truth show that you trust God?

- What if you were the only Christian in a group and others made fun of you because you love and believe in Jesus? Could you stand firm?

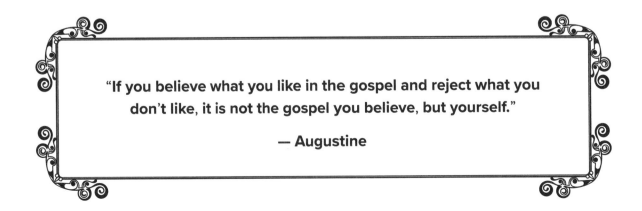

"If you believe what you like in the gospel and reject what you don't like, it is not the gospel you believe, but yourself."

— Augustine

A Woman of FORGIVENESS

Corrie's Story

Do you ever wonder what God has planned for your future? Are you sometimes impatient to find out? Do you feel thankful for the experiences God is bringing into your life today to prepare you to follow His call in the future?

When Corrie ten Boom turned 50 years old, she had not yet begun God's most challenging assignment for her. She was not married and had no children. Corrie and her sister Betsie cared for their father and worked with him in his watch repair shop.

Corrie trusted and obeyed God. She kept her heart, mind, and life open to hearing God. One of her sayings was, "Don't bother to give God instructions, just report for duty."

War

Corrie's family loved the Jewish people. Generations of her family had prayed for them. Her father invited Jews into their home for prayer and Bible study, and some trusted Jesus as their Savior.

World War II began, and Hitler's Nazis took over the Netherlands, including Haarlem, the city where the ten Boom family lived. Like Haman in Queen Esther's time, the Nazis were intent on the destruction of the Jews. The ten Booms began helping Jewish people get food and other necessities, ultimately hiding them in their home from the Nazis. After several years, the entire ten Boom family was caught and taken to prison. Corrie's father and sister Betsie died while in the concentration camp.

After her release from prison and the end of the war, Corrie helped victims of the war find healing in the love and forgiveness of Jesus. Corrie traveled to 64 countries, sharing how God taught her to forgive and have mercy toward those who mistreated and abused her and her family in prison.

Key Bible Verse:

"For if you forgive others their trespasses, your heavenly Father will also forgive you."
(Matthew 6:14)

Key Word: FORGIVENESS

Forgiveness: To give up resentment (bitterness toward someone who you feel has mistreated you)

The Netherlands

Corrie and her family lived in the Netherlands, also called Holland. The full name of the Netherlands is Kingdom of the Netherlands. The main language of the country is Dutch. Netherlands means "low country." Much of the country is below sea level. Dikes and sand dunes prevent it from flooding.

✓ **Corrie's Birth and Death**

Corrie ten Boom was born on April 15, 1892, in Haarlem, Netherlands. She died on her birthday in 1983, in Placentia, California.

✓ **Names**

Corrie's full name was Cornelia Arnolda Johanna ten Boom.

✓ **Watchmaker**

Following the tradition of her grandfather and father, Corrie became a licensed watchmaker. Corrie was distinguished in that she was not only the first female watchmaker in her family, but also in the Netherlands.

✓ **The 100-Year Prayer Meeting**

In 1844, Corrie's grandfather, Willem ten Boom, moved a prayer meeting for the Jewish people from the church he attended into his home. These prayer meetings continued for 100 years, until Feb. 28, 1944, when Nazi soldiers arrested Corrie and her entire family for harboring Jews.

✓ **Notes of Cheer**

Corrie's mother was often sick in bed. Though she was bedridden, she sent notes of cheer to others and found ways to spread God's love. She died in 1921, when Corrie was 29.

✓ **Serving God**

Before the war, Corrie and her sister Betsie cared for foster children in their home in Haarlem. Corrie taught Sunday school and Bible classes, and started clubs for teenage girls. On Sunday afternoons, she held church services for developmentally disabled people.

✓ **A Godly Sister**

Betsie was a godly example for Corrie in prison. She reminded Corrie to be thankful in all circumstances. Once when Corrie was upset about all the fleas in the prison, Betsie told Corrie to thank God for the fleas. Corrie thought it was a strange suggestion, but she followed Betsie's advice. Later, Betsie and Corrie found out why the guards never discovered the secret Bible study they held for the women in their quarters. Because the guards detested the fleas, they stayed away! Betsie had been wise to give thanks for the fleas. Betsie and their father died in prison.

✓ **Books and Movies**

Corrie wrote numerous books about her life and her spiritual journey. *The Hiding Place*, the book about how Corrie and her family hid Jews in their home, was made into a movie in 1975. Later, Corrie appeared in a movie about her life called *Corrie: The Lives She Touched*.

Dutch Words Puzzle

In the following puzzle, find the Dutch words from the list below the puzzle.
(The English words in the list are not found in the puzzle.) The words can be found
vertically (up and down) and horizontally (from left to right). Answers are in the Answer Key.

g	e	l	o	o	f	a	z	j	c	x	e	n	v	f
b	y	d	o	w	u	g	b	e	w	a	k	e	r	t
h	s	i	r	r	v	j	q	z	k	p	a	d	l	o
m	n	a	l	z	a	b	y	u	c	w	m	e	d	x
e	w	j	o	o	d	s	e	s	f	g	e	r	h	t
u	h	s	g	v	e	r	r	a	d	e	r	l	o	i
r	j	q	k	e	r	p	l	o	n	a	y	a	r	c
m	b	v	e	r	s	t	o	p	p	e	n	n	l	z
r	x	d	e	t	f	g	t	g	v	u	w	d	o	c
e	h	v	e	r	g	e	v	e	n	b	s	i	g	n
d	r	j	q	o	l	o	c	h	r	i	s	t	e	n
d	m	a	z	u	s	b	x	e	y	j	c	z	p	k
i	d	w	e	w	v	u	g	i	t	b	s	r	h	f
n	i	m	o	e	d	p	j	m	p	e	l	n	k	q
g	e	v	a	n	g	e	n	i	s	l	a	d	m	m

English	Dutch		English	Dutch
Christian	= **christen**		**sister**	= **zus**
Jesus	= **Jezus**		**trust**	= **vertrouwen**
Netherlands	= **Nederland**		**Jews**	= **Joodse**
prison	= **gevangenis**		**salvation**	= **redding**
forgive	= **vergeven**		**Bible**	= **Bijbel**
wristwatch	= **horloge**		**war**	= **oorlog**
hide	= **verstoppen**		**faith**	= **geloof**
secret	= **geheim**		**courage**	= **moed**
room	= **kamer**		**traitor**	= **verrader**
father	= **vader**		**guard**	= **bewaker**

The ten Booms hid Jewish friends in a secret place in their home.

Nazi soldiers patrolled the streets near the ten Booms' home and shop.

The Weight of Unforgiveness

Unforgiveness can weigh down our hearts and keep us from having peace. Mark 11:25 tells us that unforgiveness may even hinder our prayers. After Corrie ten Boom forgave her former persecutor, she felt God's love and peace. (See the story "Struggling to Forgive" on page 100.)

Make a paper airplane, and tape a nickel to the underside of one wing. Try to fly the plane. How well does it fly? The coins are not visible from the top, and the plane looks fine. The coin represents the resentment and unforgiveness you may feel after someone is rude to you or pushes you, or when your parents or teachers correct you.

Tape another coin to the plane and try to fly it, then still another. As resentments continue to grow, our hearts are not free to become what God has planned for us to be. Even if we look fine to others from the outside, hidden resentment is sin against God and harmful to our growth as Christians.

Make another plane, but don't tape a coin to it. How does it fly? When it's not weighed down, it is free to fulfill the purpose for which it was made — just as we, like Corrie ten Boom, are free to experience God's peace and love when we forgive others.

Make a paper airplane using a design of your choice, or follow the instructions below.

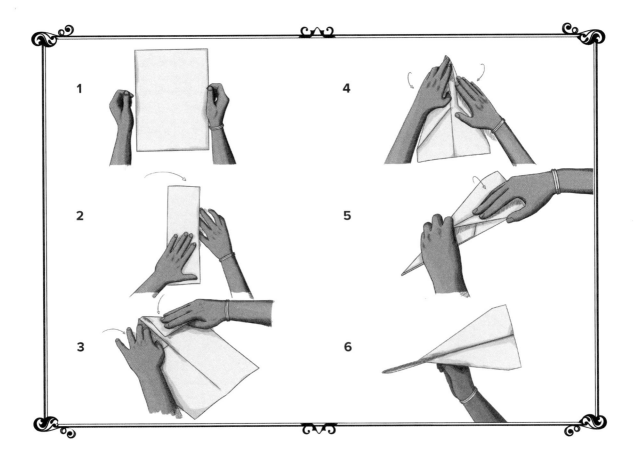

"And we know that for those who love God, all things work together for good, for those who are called according to his purpose" (Romans 8:28).

Some American kids were asked, "Why do you think Christians suffer?" Here are some of their answers:

"God knows our faith will be greatly strengthened [by suffering], and if we stand up for what we believe, we will believe it even more strongly." — Catherine, age 12

"The Bible says, 'Although he was a Son, he learned obedience from the things which he suffered.' If we are children of God walking in his steps, we will learn obedience, just like Jesus did, through suffering." — Corrie, age 12 *(not Corrie ten Boom)*

"Christians suffer so that they can learn more about God." — Rose, age 8

Corrie's Lesson

When Corrie was a child, she heard stories of Christians suffering for their faith. She worried that she would never be strong enough to suffer for her faith. Corrie's father was a wise man. He reminded her of all the times they had traveled on the train. Then he asked Corrie, "When do I give you the ticket for the trip? Three weeks before we go?"

"No," answered Corrie. "You give me the ticket right before we get on the train."

Corrie's father told her that our wise heavenly Father knows just when we are going to need things, too. "When you are called upon for the honor of suffering for Jesus, He will give you the strength you need, just in time."

What are your thoughts about suffering?

_____

_____

_____

Will you trust God to give you the strength you need "just in time?"

_____

_____

_____

Corrie ten Boom traveled around the world teaching people what she learned about faith and forgiveness during her time in prison.

"God forgives," she told the Germans after the Allied forces ended the war and Germany was defeated. She knew that was what they needed to hear.

One day after she spoke at a church in Germany, a man from the crowd approached her. Suddenly, she remembered where she had seen him before. He was one of the cruel guards who had mistreated Corrie and her sister Betsie in a German prison camp.

"I have become a Christian," the man told Corrie. "I know that God has forgiven me, but will you forgive me?" He extended his hand to her.

Corrie struggled to obey. She prayed for help to lift her hand toward his. As she put her hand in his, God provided her the strength to truly feel forgiveness for the man. Corrie was grateful for God's great grace, because she knew the verse "But if you do not forgive others their trespasses, neither will your Father forgive your trespasses (Matthew 6:15)."

Corrie asked for God's help to forgive the former prison guard. Are there any of God's commands that you feel you can't obey without His help? Will you ask Him to help you?

"Be kind to one another, tenderhearted, forgiving one another, as God in Christ forgave you."
— Ephesians 4:32

To Think About

- Are there people in the world, or groups of people, that you think God would not forgive if they asked Him for forgiveness? Is there anyone you know of that you feel you could never forgive?

- Why do you think it is hard to forgive some people?

- Does anyone deserve God's forgiveness more or less than anyone else?

John Wesley
(1703 – 1791)

A Man of GRATITUDE

John's Story

Eleven-year-old Hetty Wesley woke up about midnight. Pieces of the roof of her house were falling on her bed! And the pieces were on fire!

Hetty ran to find her parents. The family hurried out of the burning house to safety — everyone except 5-year-old John. The children's father, Samuel, tried to reach John several times, but the flames were too hot. The family knelt to pray.

Suddenly John's face popped up in an upstairs window. One neighbor stood on the shoulders of another, and they snatched John out of the house just before the roof collapsed. "Come, neighbors!" Samuel called out. "Let us give thanks to God. He has given me all my children. Let the house go; I am rich enough!" Susanna, the children's mother, called John "a brand plucked from the burning" (Zechariah 3:2).

John grew up to be a minister. He traveled to America to work with Native Americans. However, he was not very successful in his ministry. As a young minister, he made many mistakes. When he was 39, he attended a Christian meeting at which the Holy Spirit helped him understand that he could not earn his salvation. He understood that good habits are the result of God's grace and mercy, not the cause. He later wrote, "I felt my heart strangely warmed; I felt I did trust in Christ, in Christ alone, for salvation." John was grateful for God's goodness.

John became a strong leader. God used him to help in a great revival in England. Throughout the rest of his life, he traveled 250,000 miles on horseback sharing the gospel, and he preached 40,000 sermons. He is considered the founder of the Methodist and Wesleyan denominations.

When John encountered problems, he did not pray, "Lord, take this plague away from me," but "Let me be purified, not consumed." The "brand plucked from the fire" was not consumed, but lived for the glory of God.

Key Bible Verses:

"And let the peace of Christ rule in your hearts, to which indeed you were called in one body. And be thankful. Let the word of Christ dwell in you richly, teaching and admonishing one another in all wisdom, singing psalms and hymns and spiritual songs, with thankfulness in your hearts to God. And whatever you do, in word or deed, do everything in the name of the Lord Jesus, giving thanks to God the Father through him."
(Colossians 3:15–17)

Key Word: GRATITUDE

Gratitude: Thankfulness

Brand:

A burned or partly burned piece of wood

Fascinating Facts!

✓ **John's Siblings**
John's parents, Susanna and Samuel, had 19 children in 20 years, but only 10 survived.

✓ **Family Life**
Susanna Wesley, John's mother, was a minister's daughter, and her husband, Samuel, was also a minister. She had 24 siblings, so she knew how to manage a large family well. Every day, one of Samuel and Susanna's older children took a younger one aside for Bible reading and prayer time together. Every week Susanna spent 15 minutes alone with each child talking about the child's spiritual life.

✓ **Birthday Tradition**
On the day of each Wesley child's fifth birthday, Susanna spent all day with the birthday child. The child had to learn the letters of the alphabet and a prayer on that day. Most of the Wesley children, including John, did this in six hours or less.

✓ **Child Training**
Samuel, John's father, once asked Susanna how she could endure telling the children something she wanted them to learn 20 times. She said if she only told them 19 times, she would have "lost all my labor; for it was the 20th time that crowned the whole."

✓ **The Holy Club**
In college, John and his brother Charles organized the "Holy Club" to encourage Bible study, prayer, fasting, and service. Some students made fun of the group and tried to insult them by calling them "Methodists" because they had a method for all their activities.

✓ **Deeply Grateful**
John learned about true gratitude while talking one evening with a maintenance worker at his college. The man had few clothes, nothing to eat, and no bed to sleep on. However, he was deeply grateful to God for his life and for the opportunity to serve the Lord.

✓ **Famous Hymn Writer**
John's brother, Charles, wrote more than 7,000 hymns.

✓ **Farewell**
John was often heard expressing his gratitude to God during his final days when he was bedridden. His final words were, **"The best of all is, God is with us. Farewell!"**

What Are You Grateful For?

John Wesley was most grateful for God's free gift of salvation through faith in His Son, Jesus.

Challenge

"Give thanks in all circumstances; for this is the will of God in Christ Jesus for you." (1 Thessalonians 5:18)

To begin to "give thanks in all circumstances," write down five things you are thankful for each day for the next 10 days. Use the suggestions below or create your own categories. (If you have to miss a day, start again where you left off.)

Day 1: Five people who bring thoughts of gratitude to your heart (past or present):

_____

Day 2: Five places in God's creation that have been a blessing to you:

_____

Day 3: Five Bible truths or instructions that have impacted your life:

_____

Day 4: Five experiences or events you recall with delight and thankfulness:

_____

Day 5: Five things God created among all His creation for which you are grateful:

_____

Day 6: Five Christian songs that make your heart rejoice and encourage you:

_____

Day 7: Five challenging circumstances God used for good in your life:

_____

Day 8: Five Christian books or movies that have encouraged and blessed you:

_____

Day 9: Five special gifts you have received that have enriched your life:

_____

Day 10: Five specific ways your needs have been provided for each day:

_____

Think through your list each day, remembering why you are thankful. For example, if you listed a friend's name on Day 1, think about reasons you are thankful for him or her. Remember to thank God in prayer for His goodness to you!

As a child, John was rescued from his burning house as he fell into the safety of his father's arms. Later, as an adult, John learned that he could rest peacefully in the arms of his Heavenly Father, depending on Him alone for salvation.

Color each numbered shape with the color corresponding to that particular number. What image is revealed? Hint: John Wesley rode one of these more than 250,000 miles during his lifetime. The earth at the equator is 24,901 miles. How many times did Wesley travel the distance around the earth?

Do All the Good You Can

"Do all the good you can, in all the ways you can, to all the souls you can, in every place you can, with all the zeal you can." — John Wesley

John Wesley took seriously Jesus' instruction to show our gratitude to Him by feeding the hungry, visiting the sick, and welcoming strangers. (See Matthew 25:35–36.)

Set aside some time each day to "do all the good you can." Read the suggestions below, and add ideas of your own in the spaces provided. Select several ideas you can accomplish in a morning or afternoon. Then discuss your ideas with your parents to create a plan of action!

1. When you are out with your parents, be aware of anyone you could help. (For example, opening a door, returning a grocery cart to the entrance of the store, retrieving something someone dropped, helping a lost child find his or her parent, or other helpful acts.)

2. Do a chore at home without being asked.

3. Offer to help your parents, siblings, and/or grandparents accomplish a project or task.

4. Ask for permission to clean your mom's or dad's vehicle.

5. Ask for ways you could serve the younger children in your family, church, or neighborhood.

6. Write a thank-you note to your parents, grandparents, pastor, teacher, mail carrier, fireman — anyone who serves you or your family.

7. Volunteer for a local ministry or outreach.

8. Participate in outreach to needy children.

9. Offer to do yard work for a sick or elderly person or assist in other ways. (For example, families can volunteer to deliver weekly meals to sick or elderly people through community outreach.)

10. Bake cookies or homemade bread for someone who needs encouragement.

11. _____

12. _____

13. _____

14. _____

15. _____

What Do You Think?

John Wesley tried to help those who heard him preach grow as Christians and become what God wanted them to be. In his sermons, he preached about growing and maturing as a follower of Christ. What do you think about his suggestions for those who desire to grow in their faith? Write your thoughts on the lines below the following questions.

1. John Wesley said, "We should be continually laboring to cut off all the useless things that surround us." Are there objects or activities in your life that are useless to your growth as a Christian? What are some things that might help you grow?

   _____

   _____

   _____

2. John Wesley said we should be thankful for difficult things that happen to us because they help us grow in grace. Do you think it's possible to be thankful for such things? Read James 1:2–4. Why does James say we should "consider it all joy" when we experience trials?

   _____

   _____

   _____

3. John Wesley said, "proceed with much prayer" if you want God to guide your life as a Christian. Jesus said, "apart from Me, you can do nothing" (John 15:5, ESV). Besides meals, what situations in life do you begin with prayer? What are some other common situations in your day-to-day life where you need to ask for God to lead you and show you the way He wants you to "proceed"?

   _____

   _____

   _____

4. What are some other things that you think help people grow as Christians?

   _____

   _____

   _____

Talking to God

John Wesley was grateful to God for His grace, and no doubt he thanked God often for His mercy. Gratitude is an important part of prayer. But it's not the only part.

Jesus taught His disciples where to start when they talk to God. He said, "*Pray then like this: 'Our Father in heaven, hallowed be your name. Your kingdom come, your will be done, on earth as it is in heaven. Give us this day our daily bread, and forgive us our debts, as we also have forgiven our debtors. And lead us not into temptation, but deliver us from evil.* (Matthew 6:9–13)

When Jesus said this is how we should pray, He did not mean we have to pray those exact words every time we pray. Instead, He gave us a guide for how to talk to God.

So how should we pray? Remember the acronym A-C-T-S.

A = Adoration, which means praising God for who He is
C = Confession, or telling God how you have sinned and asking for forgiveness
T = Thanksgiving/Gratitude, or thanking God for what He has done in your life
S = Supplication, which is asking God for help with your needs and the needs of others

Answer the questions below to further guide you in praying. Your answers may change from day to day. You probably don't say the same words to human friends every day when you talk to them!

A: What can I praise God for?

_____

_____

C: How have I sinned against God?

_____

_____

T: What am I grateful to God for?

_____

_____

S: What do I want to ask God for?

_____

_____

Robert Thomas
(1839 – 1866)

A Man of ZEAL

Robert's Story

Robert had never felt such sadness. He and his wife, Carrie, had lost their unborn baby, and then Carrie died. They had been prepared to face anything together, but now she was gone. A few years earlier, as a young man in Wales, Robert had a promising future.

Robert preached his first sermon at age 17. Later, he was ordained as a pastor. He was zealous to take the gospel to the people of East Asia, where most had never even seen a Bible. Carrie shared his passion.

Sadly, Carrie died within five months of their arrival in China as missionaries. Robert was so grief-stricken that he stopped being a missionary for a while and got another job in China. Then Robert met two Christian traders from Korea. Few Koreans followed Jesus. Korean leaders at the time hated people and ideas from other countries.

But Robert was more zealous for lost people than he was for his own safety. When the two Korean Christians set out for their return trip to Korea, Robert joined them. Officials threatened severe punishment for anyone who talked to foreigners, but some listened to Robert's preaching and accepted his gift of a Bible anyway.

Later, Robert found a way to take the gospel to Korea, as a translator aboard a Chinese trading ship. On a trip to Korea, the ship's crew fired cannons on hostile Koreans on the shore. Fearing they would lose the battle and the Bibles would be lost, Robert threw the Bibles into the water. He managed to get some of them to the shore himself, in his final effort to reach the Koreans.

Years later, missionaries discovered that Koreans had come to Christ after reading the Bibles. Today, about one-third of South Koreans are Christian, and Christian missionaries from South Korea serve God all over the world.

Key Bible Verses:

"Do not be slothful in zeal, be fervent in spirit, serve the Lord." (Romans 12:11)

Key Word: ZEAL

Zeal: Passion, determination, devotion. An eager desire for a cause to succeed.

Wales Facts

- Wales is part of the United Kingdom, along with England, Scotland, and Northern Ireland.
- About 3 million people live in Wales.
- English and Welsh are both official languages, but almost everyone speaks English.
- Road signs are written in English and Welsh.
- Many ancient castles still stand in Wales.
- The complete Bible was translated into Welsh by the end of the 16th century.

✓ **The Hermit Kingdom**

A hermit is someone who lives alone and doesn't spend much time with other people. In Robert Thomas' time, Korea was known as the Hermit Kingdom. The leaders did not want visitors, traders, or ideas from other countries to enter Korea.

✓ **Choi**

A 12-year-old Korean boy, Choi Chi Ryang, received one of the last Bibles Robert Thomas gave away. The boy's uncle, who was with Choi when he took the Bible, then struck Robert down. For years, no one outside of Korea knew what happened next.

✓ **Hearing the Story**

More than 20 years after Robert's death, missionary Samuel Moffett landed in Korea. He and other visitors heard the story of the man who threw Bibles into the water from a burning ship. And they also met Choi Chi Ryang, now an adult. Choi's uncle used the pages of the Bible as wallpaper inside his house. Choi later bought the house, and Koreans read the wallpaper.

✓ **The Kims**

Kim Il Sung was North Korea's first leader. Pyongyang, where Robert's ship, the *General Sherman*, ended its voyage, is the capital of North Korea. It is now against the law to follow Christ there.

Hundreds of statues of Kim Il Sung are on display in North Korea. After he died in 1994, his body was put on display in a case for citizens to visit and worship. The government wants citizens to honor Kim Il Sung, his son Kim Jong Il, and his grandson Kim Jong Un more than they honor God. After Kim Jong Il died in 2011, Kim Jong Un took over as the country's leader.

Kim Il Sung
April 15, 1912 – July 8, 1994

Kim Jong Il
Feb. 16, 1941 (or 1942) – Dec. 17, 2011

Kim Jong Un
Jan. 8, 1984 –

King Sejong

Hangul, the Korean alphabet, was invented during King Sejong's reign. (Today, North Koreans call the Korean alphabet "Chosongul.") The symbols in the alphabet stand for sounds in Korean words. To form words or syllables, letters are clustered together in groups.

For example, the Korean word for school is "hakkyo" (HAHK-gyoh). To the right you can see how the letters in hakkyo are written using Korean letters and how the letters are combined to form the whole word. Can you find and circle the individual letters in the symbol for hakkyo?

ㅎ = h

ㅏ = a

ㄱ = g or k

ㅛ = yo

하 ㅛ = hakkyo (school)

What if English words were written clusters of letters (symbols). Using lowercase letters, draw what your first name might look like in the boxes below. See the example for Robert.

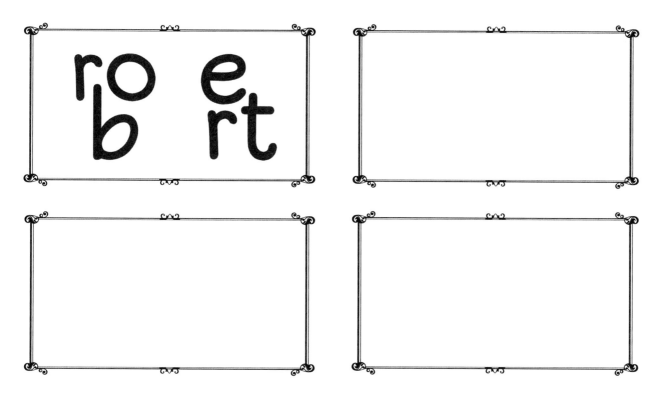

Robert cared more about the Koreans' salvation than about his own safety.

Braid a Bible Rope

In the 1800s, three Koreans went to China to find work. While they were in China, a Christian shared the gospel with them. They decided to follow Jesus! The men wondered how they could take the Good News to the people back in their home country, where it was against the law to preach the gospel.

The first two men tried to hide a Bible in their belongings and smuggle it into Korea. When they got to Korea the officials found their Bibles and executed them.

The third Christian knew he had to try something different. He carefully tore out the pages of his Bible. Then he folded each page into a narrow strip. Next he wove the strips into a long rope and tied his pack with the rope. He easily got past the guards at the border with his Bible rope. After he untied the rope and put the Bible back together, he shared the gospel wherever he went.

(Source: On This Day *by Robert J. Morgan (Nashville: Thomas Nelson, 1997)*

Cut an 8½- by 11-inch piece of paper in half lengthwise. Write or tape a copy of Genesis 1:1 in Korean on one of the halves. Fold or roll the page lengthwise into a tight narrow strip, and tape it shut. Ask someone who is good at braiding to help you braid the page into a homemade "rope," using yarn or thick string for the other two strands of the rope.

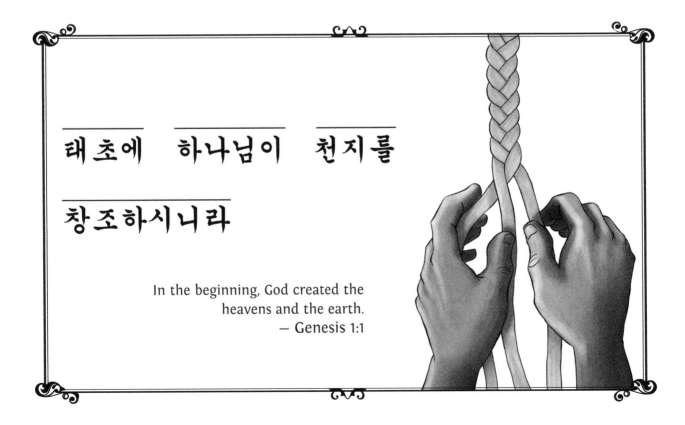

태초에 하나님이 천지를
창조하시니라

In the beginning, God created the
heavens and the earth.
— Genesis 1:1

What Do You Think?

Do you bow your head and close your eyes when you pray? Do you know why Christians do so? Many Christians believe bowing their heads and closing their eyes shows respect and humility, and is less distracting.

In North Korea, believers sometimes pray with their eyes open to keep others from knowing what they are doing. They may look at the person they are with as if they are having a conversation with them. Instead of referencing God, they may use a phrase like "Dear Leader," a title used for former leader Kim Il Sung. In this case, Christians are using the title to talk secretly about God.

Instead of bowing their heads and closing their eyes, they might look at the person sitting next to them and say, "I am so concerned about Sister Kim, who is sick. But I am thankful that our Dear Leader will show special care for her, as she needs love and attention."

What do you think?

- Is it okay for North Koreans to pray without bowing their heads and closing their eyes?

  _____

  _____

- Is it okay if they are very careful to share their faith with only a few people who might be open to hearing the gospel?

  _____

  _____

- Is it ever okay to keep your faith secret when Jesus said, "Everyone who acknowledges me before men, I also will acknowledge before my Father who is in heaven, but whoever denies me before men, I also will deny before my Father who is in heaven"? (See Matthew 10:32–33.)

  _____

  _____

- Should Robert Thomas have been more careful about how and where he shared his faith? Why or why not?

  _____

  _____

Zealous for the Lord

Shadrach, Meshach, and Abednego were zealous for the Lord. The king in their land set up a giant statue of himself and commanded everyone to bow to the image. (See Daniel 3.)

But Shadrach, Meshach, and Abednego knew that God had said, "You shall not make for yourself a carved image, or any likeness of anything that is in heaven above, or that is in the earth beneath, or that is in the water under the earth. You shall not bow down to them or serve them." (Exodus 20:4–5a)

Like Robert Thomas, the three friends were more zealous for the Lord than for their own safety. They refused to bow to the statue, even though the king threatened to throw them in a fiery furnace. In obedience to God and trusting in His wisdom, they went to the furnace. (Read what they said in Daniel 3:17–18.) God miraculously saved them from harm.

Robert Thomas also trusted and obeyed God, but his story ended differently.

Sometimes God is glorified when Christians die for their faith in Him. At other times He is glorified when He delivers people from the hands of their persecutors. No matter what, our lives are in His hands.

In the 1930s, when Japan ruled Korea, they ordered citizens to bow to Shinto idols. The rulers said even students in Christian schools must bow. The leaders of the school, like Shadrach, Meshach, and Abednego, refused to bow, and many Christian schools closed.

Today in North Korea, the people are expected to bow to statues of their leaders and to honor them as gods. Because they refuse to bow, some faithful Korean Christians are in prison, trusting God with their future and honoring Him above all.

To Talk About

- Were Shadrach, Meshach, and Abednego delivered from the flames because they had more faith than people who die for Christ? Or was His deliverance of them simply the testimony God wanted to give them?

- Read Proverbs 3:5. Will you trust God when you don't know what will happen as a result? Will you trust Him when you don't understand how He is working in others' lives through suffering or difficult times?

A Man of BOLDNESS

Martin's Story

The Luthers were one of the most highly respected families in the German town of Mansfield. Hans Luther, a hard-working and successful business owner, and his wife, Margarette, strictly disciplined their children. They were determined to raise children who would be successful as well.

Martin was born in Eisleben, Saxony, Germany, on Nov. 10, 1483. His parents sent him to school when he was 4 years old. When he grew up, Martin attended a university. In the university library, he noticed a book he had never seen before — a Bible! The book would change Luther's life.

Hans and Margarette took pride in their son's achievements at the university. They looked forward to the day when he would become a distinguished lawyer.

Martin was a brilliant student and an obedient son, but he feared he was not good enough to escape God's wrath and judgment. While caught in a violent thunderstorm one night, he was overcome by the thought that he could die with no assurance of heaven. He then vowed to God that if he survived the storm, he would join a monastery. Martin's parents were very disappointed, but he kept his vow.

Martin followed the rules of the monastery and distinguished himself as a university professor. But he feared God's judgment, and he struggled to understand the truth about salvation. Finally, after reading the Book of Romans many times, the Holy Spirit helped him understand that salvation is given by God's grace through faith in His Son, Jesus.

The church at that time told people that they could reduce the punishment for their sins by paying money to the church. Martin spoke boldly against the selling of these "indulgences." He posted his 95 Theses on the door of a church in Wittenberg, Germany, in 1517. As a result, the church was determined to punish him.

Martin stood firm in his belief in the truth of the Bible, proclaiming with boldness at his church trial, "To go against conscience is neither right nor safe. Here I stand, I can do no other."

Key Bible Verse:

"... Christ Jesus our Lord, in whom we have boldness and access with confidence through our faith in him. (Ephesians 3:11–12)

Key Word: BOLDNESS

Boldness: Courage, confidence, bravery

Monastery:

A place where monks live together in a community

Monks:

Men dedicated to religious practice, often living as a group apart from society

Theses:

Statements of opinion to be discussed

The Reformation

Martin Luther was not the only one who thought that the church of his day had drifted away from the Bible's teachings, but his boldness and persuasive written arguments brought the church's corruption into the open. He was able to spread his ideas quickly because of the recent invention of the printing press.

Protestant

Martin's desire was for the church to change its ways. But the "Reformation" he helped start soon divided the church into two separate groups: Catholics and Protestants. The new denominations that formed were called "Protestant" because they began with protests against the Catholic Church.

Outlaw

Four years after Luther posted his 95 Theses, he was excommunicated. He was condemned as a heretic and an outlaw. Fearing for his life, supporters "kidnapped" him and hid him in Wartburg Castle, where he began translating the New Testament into German.

The Most Important Book

Martin published more than 50,000 pages of Christian materials in his lifetime, yet he once said he hoped all his books would disappear and "the Holy Scriptures alone be read."

Marriage and Children

Martin helped Katharina von Bora, a former nun, escape from her nunnery in an empty fish barrel belonging to a fish merchant. Katharina was 16 years younger than Martin. No longer a monk, Martin later married Katharina and they had six children. They also cared for Martin's sister's six children.

Complete the dot to dot to reveal the great tower of Wittenberg's All Saints' Church, more commonly known as the Schlosskirche (Castle Church) in Wittenberg, Germany, where Luther nailed his 95 Theses in 1517.

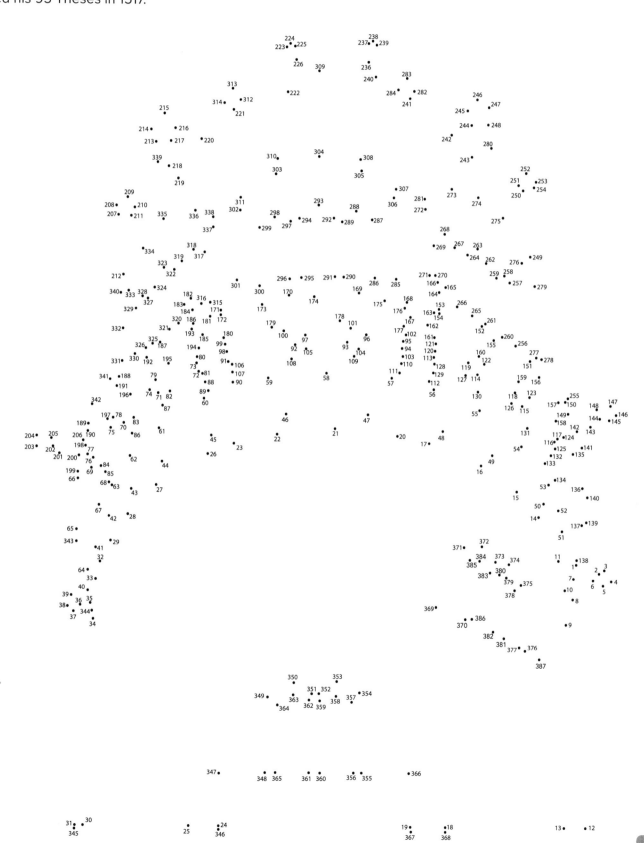

Martin nailed his 95 Theses to the door of the church.

Wartburg Castle in Thuringia, Germany, where Martin Luther was taken for his safety in May 1521. It was here that Luther translated the New Testament from Greek into German.

Martin Luther posted 95 theses on the door of the Wittenberg Castle Church. The theses were statements he believed to be true and very important.

The following are three of the theses he posted:

- "When our Lord and Master, Jesus Christ, said 'Repent,' He called for the entire life of believers to be one of repentance."

- "The true treasure of the church is the holy gospel of the glory and peace of God."

- "And let [Christians] thus be more confident of entering heaven through many tribulations [see Acts 14:22] rather than through a false assurance of peace."

> **Can you write nine theses that you believe are the truth of the Bible?**

First write three true statements about Jesus. Then write three theses that tell how God wants us to act toward other people. Finally, write three truths from Matthew chapters 5–7.

When you have finished, make another copy of your theses and ask your parent or teacher where you can post it.

1. _____

2. _____

3. _____

4. _____

5. _____

6. _____

7. _____

8. _____

9. _____

Martin Luther believed that only God's Word deserved more praise than beautiful music. "The gift of language combined with the gift of song was given to man that he should proclaim the Word of God through music," Martin said.

As a boy, Martin loved music and learned to play the lute. When he was a teenager, he made money going from house to house and serenading people.

The sale of indulgences was not the only thing Martin wanted to change about the church. Before his time, there was no congregational singing in church. Martin changed that. He also encouraged the people to sing in their own language rather than in Latin, as was the custom. His changes were considered to be very bold actions.

Hymn Writer

Martin wrote many hymns. One of his most well known hymns is "A Mighty Fortress Is Our God."

What do you think?

Do you like singing along with a group in church, or would you rather that a few people did all the singing?

_____

_____

Martin made big changes in the way music was used in church services. If you could change something about the music in your church services, what would it be?

_____

_____

Martin believed that music is a gift from God and a way to teach His truth. What are your three favorite Christian hymns or songs? What is at least one truth each song teaches?

_____

_____

What do you think is the purpose of songs that are not Christian songs? Do you think it's beneficial for Christians to play, sing, or listen to songs that don't teach Christian truths? Why or why not?

_____

_____

Boldness

Martin Luther boldly stood up for the truth when he knew he could be punished for doing so. "Boldness" is courage, confidence, and bravery. Someone who is not bold may be timid, shy, lacking in confidence, uncomfortable, or fearful.

To Think About:
Can someone feel timid and act boldly at the same time? Are there times when you are timid? Are there times when you are bold?

Put an "**S**" on the line in front of any situation in which you would be shy or timid, and a "**B**" in front of the ones in which you would be bold.

__ 1. Speaking, reading, or reciting in front of a group

__ 2. Talking to someone about your faith in Christ

__ 3. Asking your parents to go on a church mission trip

__ 4. Meeting a famous person

__ 5. Raising your hand and answering a question in a group activity or class

__ 6. Signing up for a difficult class in school

__ 7. Competing in a sport or other competition against a close rival

__ 8. Waiting for a bad storm, tornado, wildfire, or hurricane to pass

__ 9. Taking a test

__ 10. Singing or playing a solo

To Think About:

Is it wrong to be timid or uncomfortable in any of the situations on the list? Is it wise to be timid in some situations? The Bible tells us about a situation when Christians can always be bold.

And Hebrews 4:16 says, "Let us then with confidence draw near to the throne of grace, that we may receive mercy and find grace to help in time of need."

When we come to God in prayer through faith in Christ (John 14:6), we do not need to be nervous or timid. We have His assurance that He hears our prayers and understands our needs. If one of our needs is boldness in various situations, or wisdom to know when to be bold, we can ask God for that.

"... in whom we have boldness and access with confidence through our faith in him." (Ephesians 3:12)

A Man and Woman of DILIGENCE

Adoniram and Ann's Story

Thirteen days after their wedding, Ann and Adoniram Judson boarded a ship to India. The Judsons were America's first missionaries to another country.

Unable to remain in India, the Judsons sailed to Burma. Ann, who was pregnant at the time, lost their baby during the voyage. She arrived in Burma so weak and sick that she had to be carried off the boat. Adoniram and Ann were often sick because of the harsh climate. But they diligently studied the Burmese language 12 hours a day, six days a week so they could share the gospel with the Burmese people.

Ann and Adoniram trusted God and told many Burmese people about Jesus. But after the Judsons had worked in Burma for six years, not a single person had become a Christian.

Burmese people gathered in *zayats*, small huts with wide porches, to rest and talk about the news of the day. The Judsons decided to build a *zayat* by the side of a busy road. All kinds of people stopped by, including beggars, merchants, and Buddhists. They shared the truth about Jesus with anyone who would listen, and some of their visitors put their trust in Jesus!

People who did not like Christians threatened and persecuted the new Burmese believers. During a war between Britain and Burma, Adoniram was sent to prison because the Burmese leaders thought all foreigners were spies. Ann often visited officials and diligently pleaded for his release. Adoniram was finally released after 18 months. Sadly, Ann died not long after that. Adoniram was overwhelmed with grief. In spite of his sadness, he continued translating the Bible into Burmese. The entire project took more than 25 years to complete.

Adoniram worked in Burma for several more years, 37 years in all. By the time he died, in 1850, at the age of 61, there were 7,000 Christians in Burma.

Key Bible Verse:

"You shall diligently keep the commandments of the LORD your God, and his testimonies and his statutes, which he has commanded you."
(Deuteronomy 6:17)

Key Word: DILIGENCE

Diligence: Careful hard work over a period of time even in the face of difficulty or opposition, perseverance, determination, dedication

✓ A Good Student

As a child, Adoniram missed a year of school because of an illness. But he was so intelligent and diligent in his school work that he was admitted to college at age 16. He graduated at the top of his college class, and at 19 he started a school of his own in Massachusetts.

✓ Becoming a Christian

Even though Adoniram grew up as the son of a pastor, he rejected his Christian upbringing in college and became a deist. But he was unhappy. Deists believe that God created the world but doesn't have a relationship with humans or interact with them. Christians know that God is a loving heavenly Father Who cares for His children (see 1 Peter 5:7, John 3:16, and 2 Corinthians 6:18). Adoniram wholeheartedly trusted in Christ as his Lord and Savior at the age of 20.

✓ Buddhism

Most people in Burma are Buddhists. Buddhism teaches that there is no creator, no God to save them and that there is no such thing as sin to be saved from. The Judsons wanted the Buddhists to know the truth about God and Jesus.

✓ No Letters

Ann and Adoniram did not get any letters from America until they had been gone for almost four years.

✓ Hidden Treasure

Adoniram had translated part of the Bible into Burmese before he went to prison. The story is told that Ann sewed the Burmese Bible manuscripts into a pillow to hide and protect them. She smuggled the pillow into Adoniram's prison, and he slept on it. Adoniram was separated from his treasure when officials transferred him to another prison. A guard in the old prison threw the pillow away, but a Burmese Christian found it and safely returned it to the Judsons. (Color these scenes on pages 128–29.)

✓ Hard Work

Ann and Adoniram ministered in Burma for 12 years to bring 18 Burmese to Christ. Today there are an estimated 4.8 million Christians in Burma (Myanmar).

✓ A Living Sacrifice

Missionary life sometimes requires the ultimate sacrifice: Ann Judson died at age 37, Adoniram's second wife, Sarah, died at age 41, and his third wife, Emily, died at 36.

A Difficult Language

The following is John 3:16 in Burmese.

ဘုရားသခင်၏သားတော်ကို ယုံကြည်သောသူအပေါင်းတို့သည်၊ ပျက်စီးခြင်းသို့မရောက်၊

ထာဝရ အသက်ကို ရစေခြင်းငှါ၊ ဘုရားသခင်သည် မိမိ၌ တပါးတည်းသော သားတော်ကို စွန့်

တော်မူသည်တိုင်အောင် လောကီသားကို ချစ်တော်မူ၏။။

Try to copy the Burmese verse over the outline below.

ဘုရားသခင်၏သားတော်ကို ယုံကြည်သောသူအပေါင်းတို့သည်၊

ပျက်စီးခြင်းသို့မရောက်၊ ထာဝရ အသက်ကို ရစေခြင်းငှါ၊

ဘုရားသခင်သည် မိမိ၌ တပါးတည်းသော သားတော်ကို စွန့်တော်မူ

သည်တိုင်အောင် လောကီသားကို ချစ်တော်မူ၏။။

Now look up the verse in an English Bible and write it below.

_____

_____

_____

Adoniram Judson translated the Bible into the Burmese language. The work was extremely difficult. At that time, Burmese had no capital letters or punctuation and had no spaces between words, sentences, or paragraphs.

Be an Encourager

The Judsons worked diligently for the Lord in Burma, but they were discouraged from time to time by obstacles and setbacks. Electronic mail was not yet invented, and they sometimes went years without getting mail.

Today it is much easier to encourage people who serve the Lord. Can you send an encouraging message to a pastor, Sunday school teacher, short- or long-term missionary, Christian musician, church maintenance worker, Christian writer or blogger, military chaplain, or other Christian worker?

Use the example below to guide you, or write or email a message of your own.

Dear _____,

My name is _____, and I am _____ years old. I would like to

thank you for serving the Lord by (see *1 suggestions below) _____.

Your faithfulness is a good example. I hope you will be encouraged by this Bible verse:

(see *2 suggestions below) _____

I will pray that (see *3 suggestions below) _____.

Sincerely,

_____

*1.   **a.** preaching the gospel faithfully; **b.** serving our church; **c.** being willing to travel to share the love of Jesus; **d.** (another description)

*2.   **a.** And let us not grow weary of doing good, for in due season we will reap, if we do not give up. (Galatians 6:9); **b.** And how are they to preach unless they are sent? As it is written, "How beautiful are the feet of those who preach the good news!" (Romans 10:15); **c.** Casting all your anxieties on him, because he cares for you. (1 Peter 5:7); **d.** (another verse you choose)

*3.   **a.** God will bless you and your family; **b.** God will give you wisdom in every situation; **c.** you will be strong in the Lord; **d.** (another prayer)

Ann and Adoniram Judson noticed that the people in Burma enjoyed the custom of gathering in *zayats* to rest and talk. After the Judsons built their own *zayat*, people began to listen to them talk about Jesus.

What is an unwritten rule? Why does it make a difference if missionaries and other visitors follow local customs?

_____

_____

_____

How can you help new people in your church or Sunday school class who may not know your customs? How could you help non-Christian visitors who may not know anything about Christian teachings?

_____

_____

_____

What are some unwritten rules or customs in your country that others may have trouble understanding? For example, how do you greet people? (If you know people from other countries, ask how they greet people in their country and what customs they find unusual in your country.)

_____

_____

_____

Different Customs

A visitor to the United States from another country said, "To my people, the more you go and visit someone in their house (even surprise visits), the more they like you. To the American, the more you go visit someone (especially surprise visits), the more irritating you are to them."

Adoniram Judson drifted away from Christian teachings when he went to college. As a teenager, Ann Judson thought mostly about going to parties and having a good time. Later, Adoniram and Ann became diligent about their faith and committed themselves to following God.

It's not easy to lead a Christian life, continually falling short of God's righteousness while trusting in Christ's work of redemption. If we don't make it a priority to practice our faith and hide God's Word in our hearts, we can be easily led astray by unbiblical cultural influences and ideologies.

What are some of the ways you can strengthen your faith?

1. Pray and ask God to help you grow in your faith.

2. If you have questions about God or about Bible teachings, ask your parents to answer them, or search out the answers in the Bible together.

3. Listen to pastors in church and teachers in Sunday school. Every week, share with your family three things you learned from their teachings.

4. Read the Bible often. Ask your parents to suggest a reading plan for you.

5. Read other Christian books and biographies of faithful Christians.

6. Teach younger children about being a follower of Jesus by helping in Sunday school or Vacation Bible School. Study what you plan to teach them to be sure you understand it, too.

"Be watchful, stand firm in the faith, act like men, be strong. Let all that you do be done in love."
(1 Corinthians 16:13–14)

Answer & Color Keys

Page 7

Jim Elliot's Famous Quote
"He is no fool who gives what he cannot keep to gain what he cannot lose."

Page 8

PAGE 9

Page 15

Bible Verse Cryptogram from Romans 5:3–4 (NIV)
We also glory in our sufferings, because we know that suffering produces perseverance; perseverance, character; and character, hope.

The Answer Key and larger
images of coloring pages
may be viewed at
www.torchlighters.co

THE INTERPRETER'S HOUSE

SALVATION HILL

THE HOUSE BEAUTIFUL

THE CELESTIAL CITY

THE GATE

THE VALLEY OF HUMILIATION

GALITY HILL

THE SWAMP OF DESPONDENCY

APOLLYON'S LAIR

THE PLEASANT HILLS

VANITY FAIR

THE CITY OF DESTRUCTION

CASTLE DESPAIR

In the *dust of defeat* as well as the laurels of *Victory* THERE IS A GLORY to be found if one has done HIS BEST.

The Answer Key and larger
images of coloring pages
may be viewed at
www.torchlighters.co

Morse Code Quote

God will judge us not according to
how much we endured, but
how much we loved.

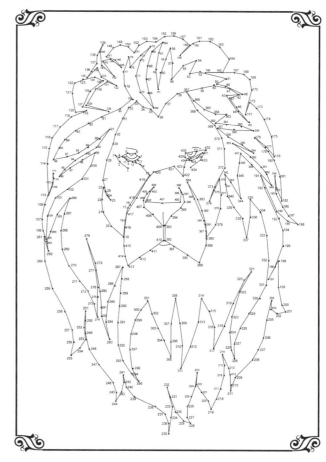

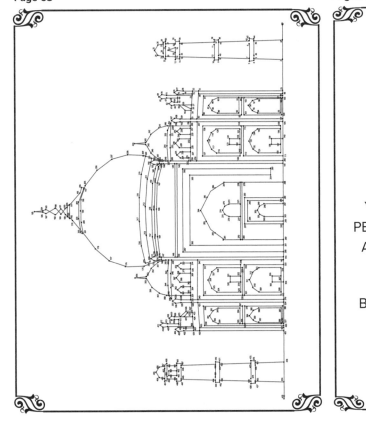

What William Said

GOD SHALL HAVE ALL THERE IS OF
WILLIAM BOOTH.

YOU CANNOT WARM THE HEARTS OF
PEOPLE WITH GOD'S LOVE IF THEY HAVE
AN EMPTY STOMACH AND COLD FEET.

BELIEVE WITH ALL YOUR MIGHT ALL HE
HAS SAID IN HIS HOLY WORD.

- Algeria
- Democratic Republic of the Congo (DRC)
- Sudan
- Libya
- Chad
- Niger
- Angola
- Mali
- South Africa
- Ethiopia
- Mauritania
- Egypt
- Tanzania
- Nigeria
- Namibia
- Mozambique
- Zambia
- South Sudan
- Somalia
- Central African Republic (CAR)
- Madagascar
- Botswana
- Kenya
- Cameroon
- Morocco

The Answer Key and larger images of coloring pages may be viewed at **www.torchlighters.co**

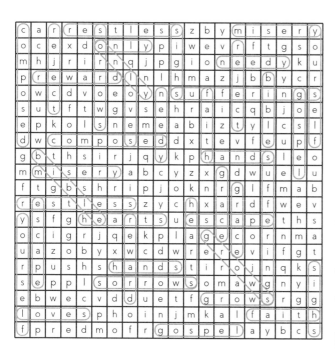

g	e	l	o	o	f	a	z	j	c	x	e	n	v	f
b	y	d	o	w	u	g	b	e	w	a	k	e	r	t
h	s	i	r	r	v	j	q	z	k	p	a	d	l	o
m	n	a	l	z	a	b	y	u	c	w	m	e	d	x
e	w	j	o	o	d	s	e	s	f	g	e	r	h	t
u	h	s	g	v	e	r	r	a	d	e	r	l	o	i
r	j	q	k	e	r	p	l	o	n	a	y	a	r	c
m	b	v	e	r	s	t	o	p	p	e	n	n	l	z
r	x	d	e	t	f	g	t	g	v	u	w	d	o	c
e	h	v	e	r	g	e	v	e	n	b	s	i	g	n
d	r	j	q	o	l	o	c	h	r	i	s	t	e	n
d	m	a	z	u	s	b	x	e	y	j	c	z	p	k
i	d	w	e	w	v	u	g	i	t	b	s	r	h	f
n	i	m	o	e	d	p	j	m	p	e	l	n	k	q
g	e	v	a	n	g	e	n	i	s	l	a	d	m	m

Pages 96 – 97

Page 104

Page 105

Page 119

Page 120

The Answer Key and larger
images of coloring pages
may be viewed at
www.torchlighters.co

Pages 128 – 129

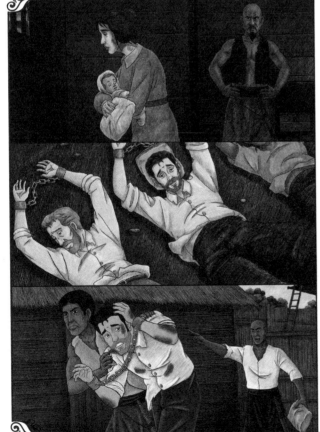

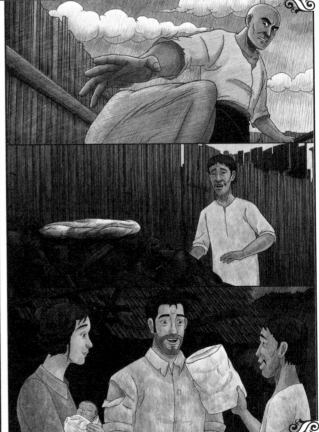